MAKING GAME:
AN ESSAY ON WOODCOCK

**"WOODCOCK MOON:
NORTHERN MICHIGAN"**
Acrylic on board
Russell Chatham

MAKING GAME:
AN ESSAY ON WOODCOCK

By Guy de la Valdene
frontspiece and illustrations by Russell Chatham

WILLOW CREEK PRESS

ACKNOWLEDGEMENTS

I am indebted to the following for their help and patience: Mr. Tom Dwyer, Section Migratory Game Birds, Patuxent Wildlife Research Center, Laurel, Maryland; Mr. Peter B. Devers of the New York State Falconry Association; The National Sporting Library, Middleburg, Virginia; Mr. Lou Razek, Highwood Farms Bookshop, Traverse City, Michigan; Mrs. Pamela Grath, Kalamazoo, Michigan; Mr. Tom Nouveau, Deadrock, Montana.

ISBN 0-932558-21-6

*This book is dedicated
to the memory of Essie.*

CONTENTS

The woods are for the hunters of dreams. . .

Sam Walter Foss (1858-1911)
The Bloodless Sportsman

FOREWORD

My woodcock appeared on a gilded plate, alongside a
sprig of watercress and a shock of straw-colored french
fries. He sat with his head tucked under his wing on top
of a square of toasted white bread over which was spooned a dark purée. The French waiter ceremoniously swept
away my empty soup bowl and neatly replaced it with
"une bécasse pour monsieur." I was ten years old.

It looked okay, a little like squab, except that for some
ungodly reason someone had forgotten to dispatch its
head. Not knowing what to do, I looked to my father for
guidance. He had selected a species of perch, a prisoner
of the deep waters of Lac d'Anecy, and had already
deboned it. He laughed and advised, "Pretend you're
Robespierre and cut it off. Then if you feel ambitious,
pinch its bill and bite off the top of its head. The brain is
what you want." It was an ambition I did not share, but
the bird was delicious. I finished it with my fingers,
much to the disapproval of the waiter. Visible through
the nuisance of a few bones was a hunting scene baked
into the plate, depicting a Gordon setter on point and a
farm girl reclining on a haystack with her thumb in her
mouth. I discovered the woodcock, nestled beneath her

petticoats in the swale of a thigh. Facing me at the bottom of the plate, the inscription read *"Quelle bécasse!"* In France addled young girls are sometimes called *bécasses.*

My father congratulated me. "Didn't think you'd eat the toast and trail."

"Trail?"

"Insides. You know -- the intestines."

"You mean the 'caca?' "

He laughed. He loved to laugh, and he loved good food, but he didn't like to hunt. He'd done that in airplanes for three years in one war and twenty-five years later as a member of the Free French. He wouldn't shoot things that didn't shoot back. He's dead now. I've never been to war, and I bird-hunt.

I wrote this book for two reasons: First, I was interested in finding out more about a bird I hunt every fall, and secondly, I hoped that I would resolve my reasons for hunting in the first place. I accomplished the first and failed in the second.

My research took a year, and I used it as an excuse to follow a migration and see the country. During those months I met and corresponded with some very dedicated men and women. I also ran headlong into the cogwheels of government.

I began hunting at the age of seven. Thirty years later I regret the finality of it but know that whatever the ancestral urge is, it is very much with me. The morality behind hunting is buried beneath a dozen reasons, all of which are valid, but none of which ultimately satisfy. me. It wouldn't occur to me to harm an animal unless I were actively hunting it. I condemn cruelty of any kind, and yet I have crippled more birds than most. The contradictions are hyprocritical, but, even though I cannot explain them, I do not feel like a hypocrite. What I am is a bird-hunter, and for sanity's sake I will leave it at that.

The main thrust of the state and federal wildlife agencies is directed towards game of major interest to the public, i.e., ducks, pheasants and geese. Other game birds are referred to as "secondary species."

This book tells the story of a secondary species, an odd, reclusive bird who delights those who see him and fascinates those who study him. Scientists key his progression from the class of *Aves* to the genus and species of *Scolopax minor*. We know him as the American woodcock.

PROLOGUE

The woodcock landed shortly before daybreak in a clearing surrounded by half a dozen barren tamarack trees adjoining a sphagnum swamp, just one mile from where he had been born. He was tired and hungry. The seventy-mile leg from Alligator Lake to Calais, Maine had taken all night and almost his life. A long-eared owl had been waiting, and the woodcock distinctly remembered the swirl of cold air and the plaintive cry of his travelling companion. He hadn't wanted to fly against the blustery night wind, but something had made him do it, something that told him he was close to a correct intercept of latitude and longitude. Tired as he was, there was a familiarity about the area that dissipated the burden of the past three weeks. He ruffled his feathers and set about preening. His two companions from the journey's start would not compete with him for attention. One had flown into a telephone wire and fluttered headless to the ground on the outskirts of a small town in eastern Tennessee, and the other had perished in the talons of the owl. The woodcock finished smoothing his feathers and removed a small piece of grass caught between his leg and the tarnished metal band he'd worn all his life. The band didn't bother him except occasionally when debris got caught beneath it. He walked a few feet, listened, and probed unsuccessfully in the ground. The temperature was thirty-eight degrees Fahrenheit, and the earth was hard. This last day of March reminded him of fall.

ONE

I've always assumed that all birds mated and were
born in the spring. I suppose I wanted it to be that way.
I was wrong, but I still choose to believe that life -- all
life -- hatches from womb and egg in May. It's a fine
month, and it's simpler to think of it that way.

Spring starts early for woodcock and is a confusing
time of the year because although they winter in the
South, the birds are opportunistic by nature and are content as long as the earth remains soft to stay just ahead
of the weather. A freeze urges them further and further
down the continent until, as in the case of Louisiana,
land gives way to water. Mild winters, on the other
hand, upset their metabolism, prompting a premature
swelling of the males' testes and an irrational urge to fly
north and be the first to claim a piece of real estate.
Often those urges spell disaster. If the breeding grounds
are frozen, there will be little if any food available. Some
will die, a few will turn back, and still others will make
do, feeding as best they can alongside riverbeds and
creek bottoms. The urge to mate takes its toll on every
species.

Because of atmospheric conditions, it is difficult to pinpoint the exact date that spring begins for woodcock. It may be as early as February in the mid-northern states and as late as the second week in April in Ontario and Quebec. One thing is certain, however -- spring begins for the males the moment they arrive on the breeding grounds. Cleverly waiting for good weather and for their prospective mates to work out their territorial differences, the females arrive a week or two later.

Physically, woodcock appear portly. I observed one years ago, strutting across a sandy two-track, chest thrust outward, tail fanned, bobbing lasciviously up and down like a bullfrog, and I expected him to pitch over and impale his bill in the ground. I'm told that this behavior is a sign of nervousness, but in his case it was certainly disguised with élan.

In hand, the bird is a delight. From the crown of his head to the tip of his tail, his orbicular shape fits as if he'd been born to be palmed. Gauguin might well have painted him, cupped as an offering in the hands of a girl.

He is born with a long, thin bill specially designed for probing. This bill, which at first glance appears ungainly, is a wonder of engineering. Averaging two and three-quarters inches in length, it is a delicate organ, combining taste, touch and smell. The tip, which is slightly bulbous and overlaps the lower mandible, concentrates a miasma of delicate blood vessels and nerve endings that act as underground antennae in the detection of worms. Woodcock are born with a prehensile bill; a specific bone and musculature permits him to open the anterior third of his upper mandible, push dirt aside and seize his prey. The bird grasps and extracts worms between his tongue and the underside of his upper bill, which bear the rugosity of sharkskin.

His nostrils are set high against his skull, presumably to enable him to feed without impacting his nasal cavities. His ears, instead of framing both sides of his head, are situated anteriorly and a bit beneath his eyes. The eyes in turn are proportionately larger than most birds' and set very high and to the rear of his skull. His sight is acute, and his range includes lateral, posterior and overhead vision. His eyes are also black and limpid, not eyes to dwell on if one intends to keep hunting. Over the millenia, while the woodcock's bill grew and his legs shortened, his eyes travelled backwards, forcing his brain to rotate on its axis to a unique upside-down position. This linear progression of sensory organs indicates that much of his skull is geared to the task of feeding.

When I started this book, the accepted Latin name for

the American woodcock was *Philohela minor,* which translated into "little lover of the bogs." A year later the taxonomists changed the name back to *Scolopax minor.* Since 1788 the bird has been assigned no fewer than ten different generic names. The American woodcock is related to one of six families of shorebords. His is the family of Scolopacidae, which includes willets, curlews, sandpipers, plovers and others. In his case, although evolution urged him to the woods, like his cousin the snipe he retained his ancestral habits of probing and thus was rewarded with a long list of sobriquets that I won't dwell on except for one, and only because it applies to a subspecies I find offensive. Years ago it was believed that woodcock fed by sucking mud through their bills, and therefore in certain regions they were given the name of "bog suckers." An insulting assertion, but one that does deserve its place on the brass mastheads of most environmental agencies.

The woodcock's plumage deserves special attention. Overall, it is not unlike the color of a freshly killed brown trout or the skin of certain reptiles, but a glance at medieval North Africa or the presence of a seventeenth-century Flemish canvas also reminds one of the subtle beauty that exudes from this relic of another

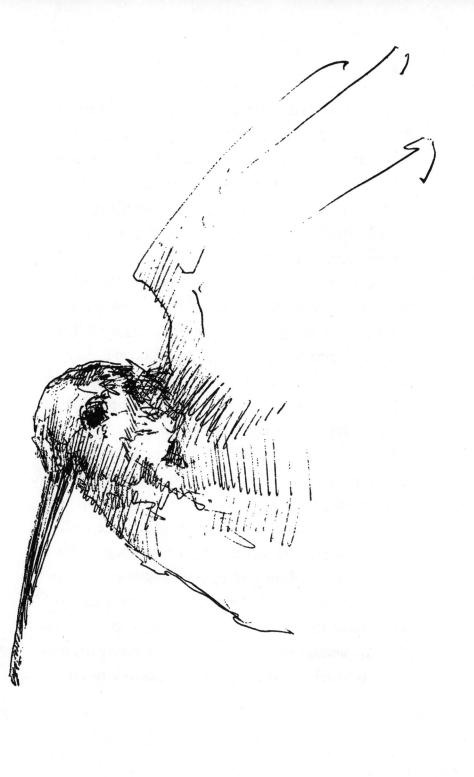

age whose survival depends on camouflage. Both male and female have identical coloration, and, except when young or during the molt, it remains constant throughout the seasons. The feathers, woven like braclets on an artichoke, are at times suffused and at other times notched, barred, edged and tipped in kaleidoscopic patterns, incredibly specific and purposeful.

Woodcock sport a cream-colored jabot around the throat and a cinnamon tea apron over breast and abdomen. A sweeping black stroke runs from the bill, surrounds the eyes and tapers close to the occiput, next to four lateral ochre crossbars that sit above a Payne grey forehead. A second but smaller signature appears lower on the cheek, darkly encasing his ears.

The base of the neck and back is mottled in burnt umber and black, except for four lines of slate grey. Two of those lines run from either side of the neck, forming two sides of a triangle ending at the cant of the back, while the others hug a straight line to the base of the wing. Paintings of the bird in flight and from the rear usually depict him lightly stamped with the letter "M." The base of the tail feathers is warm grey, giving to mottled raw sienna tipped with black. The underpart, particularly visible when the bird fans, reflects a prismatic sheen tinged in white-cream. The wings are mottled silver-grey to burnt umber near the body cavity and slowly darken to a uniform brown at the tips. A thin line of slate bisects the entirety of the wings to the primaries, while the upper part of the leg is covered in fine auburn down.

Everyone's perceptions of colors differ and vary with respect to light and taste. Some find woodcock dull compared to other species. I find that bruised peaches, reflections of gravel creeks, and the whip of red foxes evoke his memory. But then so does Pan.

Woodcock weights vary between the sexes and at different times of the year. The male bird averages a little under five and a half ounces, with lows of four ounces and highs reaching slightly over six. The female, approximately a third larger, may approach eight ounces in the fall and five in the spring. Both sexes are underweight when they return from the wintering grounds, and it appears that the northerly spring migration is intense and more demanding than the fall's flight south.

Most people I hunt with, as well as the professionals I have talked to, believe that they can tell a male from a female on the wing as well as in hand, and so do I -- but after going over the records the assumption is presumptious. There is enough of an overlap of weight to confuse. Research in the matter has culminated in a twofold measure for identification. On one hand, the bill of the female generally exceeds that of the male by a quarter of an inch (2½ to 2¾ inches), and secondly, the female's outer primaries are wider than those of the male. In the first test the overlap of confusion between the sexes ranges from 15% to 20%, but by measuring primary feathers it is reduced to 3%. Combining both differentials brings the error factor down to one-third of one percent, a figure scientists can live with.

Wings also permit a scientific evaluation of age. Examination of the tips of the bird's primaries enables one to gauge wear, thus determining if the bird has molted. If it hasn't, the woodcock is a yearling. Macroscopic examination of the secondary feathers focuses on subtle changes in color patterns indicative of age progression. The thousands of wings sent each year by hunters to the Patuxent Research Center in Laurel, Maryland, are examined both for age and sex, the adult to yearling ratio enabling the Fish and Wildlife Service to gauge annual productivity.

The insides of woodcock are simple and efficient. Like all birds, they swallow food whole rather than chew it.

The woodcock's throat leads to an underdeveloped crop, which rapidly conveys nourishment through a small tube to a muscular compartment in the stomach, where food is digested and expedited to the intestines. The process from ingestion to evacuation is a rapid one, so rapid in fact that it brings to mind the words of a somewhat fastidious French hunter and gourmet of the past who delighted in cooking his woodcock intact, trail and all. He maintained that the bird, if killed on the first flush, was a delicacy; on the second, less so; and if missed at that point should be abandoned, as it would have by then evacuated its flavor and be but a bland facsimile of itself.

In 1860 the enigmatic outline of a single feather was found imprinted in a limestone quarry in Solnhofen, Bavaria. It had not seen daylight in over a hundred and forty million years, back during the Age of Dinosaurs. This find was named "Ancient Bird" and became one of the links proving Darwin's theory of evolution. Three hundred and fifty million years ago, fish became the first vertebrates. A hundred and fifty million years after that, evolution transformed some of these fish into reptiles. The urge to fly didn't take long, as proved by the fossil of "Ancient Bird." The scales of reptiles are made of keratin, the same substance as feathers. Proof of the early existence of woodcock came from a fossil found in Florida, dating that bird to the middle of the Pleistocene Epoch, othewise known as the Age of Glaciers, or approximately one and a half million years ago. One might well speculate the beginning of Avian migration to this period, as extensive ice sheets and glaciers formed and retreated over the continent, displacing and regrouping species such as *Scolopax minor* back and forth from the boreal forests to the Southern lowlands.

As airfoils, feathers are unsurpassed. They are made of a central shaft of keratin, fringed with branches and smaller filaments attached to each other by tiny hooks. The whole is united into a curved, dovetailing vane, splendidly designed to act as an insulator, both to keep out the cold and to insure that the least amount of energy is lost during migration. The thousand or so feathers that make up the plumage of a woodcock are precisely laid out to keep him inconspicuous, warm and streamlined in flight. They do require maintenance, and like most birds he conditions them by dipping his beak in an oil gland located near the base of his tail, anointing them individually, and combing them in a ritual of toiletry similar to that of females of our species, but for different reasons. The woodcock's wings are broad and rounded, an evolutionary transformation not unlike that of his legs, which are short and plump at the thigh. His weight to wing-area ratio is small and undoubtedly facilitates migration, as short, rounded wings are better suited for dodging and swerving than for long-distance flying. The bird's breast is fleshy and made mostly of wing muscles attached to a deep keel on his breastbone. Like all flying birds, his lungs extend into air sacs which fill the space inside his breast for buoyancy.

The Seneca Indians believed that the Creator made the woodcock from the leftover parts of every other bird. If that is true, his heart must be that of the eagle, for it is big and filled with the unique courage required to wander in solitude through the mysterious forests of his continent.

Spring probes the imagination by tacking from gloom to color, from apathy to the naiveté of revery, and by insinuating an inkling of clarity into the dull haze of hibernation. Her promise of life, of revelry, of natural beauty is deliberate, sometimes palpaple, other times so faint as to be mistaken for a passing fancy. Her curtain may loiter in midstream, only to reopen momentarily on the breast of a goldfinch or descend under the weight of a

grey rain, all the time uprooting and tempting, taunting and promising the inevitable, until one morning, for no apparent reason, dawn sighs and a flushed breath of air warms the earth. Spring is the breakfast of the year.

I arrived in Lake Leelanau, Michigan, three weeks after the woodcock. Having lived in southern Florida for the better part of two decades, I had forgotten about spring. Where I live it's a short eclosion, a time of gardenias, wind and tourists. The French say, *"Plus ça va, plus c'est la même chose"* ("The more it goes, the more it's the same"), an accurate description of spring in south Florida.

Lake Leelanau was my first stop on a drive that would take me north to Sault Ste. Marie, across Canada to Rivière du Loup, south through New Brunswick to Calais, Maine, and down the Eastern Seaboard back to Florida. The purpose of the trip was to observe the woodcock's courtship, band as many broods as possible, and generally learn to think of and view the bird in a light other than fall's. Jim Harrison, poet and bon vivant, lives with his family in Lake Leelanau, and I have been their guest every October for twelve years. It was only natural that I should return to an area I knew and to a house that felt kin to mine. My travelling companion was my Labrador bitch. It was unthinkable to leave her behind, particularly as I was returning to the first place we had hunted together a decade ago.

The search for spring birds was a long one, covering some six thousand miles in three weeks, but I like to drive. It's relaxing and reminds me of cooking. Flying reminds me of nightmares. Anyway, things always happen on the road. For example, exactly sixty miles south of Macon, Georgia, on I-75, I found a Chinese restaurant that serves Peking duck. In Kentucky a bootlegger punched out a highway patrol officer in the men's room of the rest stop and was apprehended an hour later next to a flowering dogwood on the outskirts of Lexington. In a motel dining room in Indiana I eavesdropped on tragedy unfolding at a table next to mine. A very old dog trainer, wearing a tarnished whistle around his neck, was being coerced by his wife and sister into an operation. His granddaughter, or perhaps his great granddaughter, stared at her plate and whispered to him about her dog. The women, volunteer workers at the local hospital, discussed the application of detergents to third-degree burns, and the old man dropped a breaded shrimp on his cardigan. He spooned sugar into his tea, but, sugar being what it is to health, his wife cackled, replaced his cup with hers, and pressed the issue. "There's a new Italian doctor in town." Receiving no answer, she continued in a shrill voice, "I'm telling you, Henry, there is nothing to worry about." Henry replied softly, "It's my gall bladder." He coughed and lit a cigar. His sister, a large woman with too many chins, tore the cigar out of his hand and disdainfully dropped it in his water glass. The old man looked to his grandchild for credibility and burst into tears.

After two days of travel, I arrived in Lake Leelanau, and at exactly 9:01 p.m., I saw my first woodcock. The bird's nasal cry, described by some as a "peent," greeted me the moment I opened the car door. His call over-powered the itching noises of the night. Grey clouds darkened the sky in metronomed increments, and in a whistle of feathers the outline of the bird appeared out of the obscurity of the field into the thin, pale horizon. At tree level he accelerated perpendicularly, trilling and dancing with heartsick abandon, spiraling in ever-wider arches until he vanished into the clouds. Moments later I watched as he quietly glided down next to a bush in the middle of his field. His peenting resumed immediately, a three hundred and sixty degree proclamation of love and warning. At dawn and dusk every night for the next six weeks he would prance under the stars, sometimes, as in the case of a full moon, extending his affairs until first light. Back in the car, Nick Reems, a friend and hunting companion, told me that his six-year-old son insisted that he be taken to watch the woodcock fly every night. Nick seemed pleased.

Jim Harrison's house is full of books, paintings, cats and dogs. Its belly is the celler, and its heart the kitchen. We have been friends a long time, a friendship Balzacian by nature that prompts us out of bed with food on our minds, attracts us to European novels, wines and the ever-intriguing variances in women. We look forward to autumn, to our seasonal dependence on dogs, fine guns, and the making of game.

The winter of 1983 was a mild one, and I had received a call from Nick Reems on March seventeenth, announcing that birds were singing in the fields. He called again a week later, this time his breast full of beer, informing me that a massive cold front had lumbered in from Canada, turning back the clock, and that he had found a single frozen egg in a deserted nest. He was concerned for the welfare of the birds, was considering dropping several tons of earthworms from a B-52, and in a fit of melancholy had thawed, fried and eaten the egg.

Population surveys of migratory game birds are primitive but critical to their management. Conventionally, as in the case of geese and ducks, the surveys are conducted by selected area counts throughout migratory paths or in specific locales where birds are concentrated. Because of the woodcock's cryptic coloring, reclusive nature and fondness for dense diurnal cover, the usual counting methods are not applicable. Instead, the U.S. Fish and Wildlife Service (FWS) relies on singing grounds to provide an index of the breeding population.

Each spring male woodcock are counted along permanent routes randomly selected throughout the northern breeding range. Observers follow paths approximately three and a half miles long, stopping every three minutes to record the number of singing birds. Males generally begin courting a few minutes after sundown and continue for half an hour to forty-five minutes. These times fluctuate during heavy cloud cover, rain, or during the full moon. The average number of males per route is used as the index of breeding population, and from that is derived a census of the general well-being of the species.

I suspect that the FWS would like nothing better than to formulate a system that does not rely on comparable singing grounds data, as the present assessing procedure is complicated, time-consuming, and results in subjective data. What these surveys do is measure the fluctuation of breeding males in specific areas; they cannot be used as an estimate of the total number of woodcock in North America. The answer to that specific question is a vague "between six and eighteen million."

Two additional methods quoted as part of the overall census are tabulations of yearly estimates of birds killed in each state and a multiplication of that number by approximately four. Unfortunately, estimates of harvested birds rely on the number of wings sent in by hunters for analysis, and most hunters don't bother. It is also estimated a hundred acres of suitable cover will support a brace of breeding birds in the spring and a total of five in the fall prior to migration. With the help of aerial and satellite photography, the FWS can locate and measure good habitat and then apply an equation resulting in a possible, if not probably, total number of birds per state. Again, these methods rely on conjecture.

To scientists, woodcock represent a taxing challenge; to me, the very fact that they puzzle the best of them is but another of the bird's charms. Enigmas are revitalizing. Solutions, on the other hand, proclaim conclusions and are often depressing.

Jim and I followed Nick and his shorthair for two
afternoons, unsuccessfully looking for broods and
prepared only in the sense that we carried pliers, bands
and a cooler full of drinks. We didn't know what to look
for. The trees were bare and the ground soft, but in the
newness of spring the leaves were uniform in color. Off
in the distant fields a pastel hue was beginning to form
on the popples. There was a noteworthy absence of
smell; unlike fall, when rotting ferns permeate the
woods, there was a confusing freshness to the air. The
dog kept looking to us, no doubt wondering where the
guns were.

Every night after dinner I returned to the singing
fields, looking for patterns. I didn't find any, except that
the birds flew and alighted close to the same spot each
time. Waiting until they were airborne, I got close
enough to see them on the ground and to hear the soft
gurgle emitted between peents, but although on occasion
I flushed a second bird, I couldn't tell if it was a female
or a competitor. My hearing is poor, and I could not
detect the soft musical warbles that I know woodcock
give off during their dances. I did notice, though, that
the flights were dissimilar. Sometimes the birds flew in

rigid patterns, while at other times they would crochet the sky in a series of parentheses. Most birds peented a dozen or more times before flying, but others called over a hundred times. One bird I approached flew only once but peented for the better part of forty minutes. Cold and vexed, I flushed him before leaving.

It was a frustrating time for the woodcock. With a regularity matching that of the tides flowing and ebbing out of the St. Croix River, his hopes rose and fell with the moon. Just before sunset he would leave the alders bordering the pond in search of an unoccupied field, flying low over a pair of Canada geese and keeping the eagles in sight. In the three weeks since his arrival, he had witnessed the eagles building their nest, the geese taking turns incubating their eggs, those eggs hatch, and the drowning of one of the goslings in the beak of a snapping turtle.

Earlier in the month the woodcock had travelled back and forth, looking for the right opening, criss-crossing over thousands of acres of forest in the process but finding every field occupied. At first he simply landed and began peenting, but the moment he did the resident flew at him uttering a harsh, threatening "Cac-cac-cacs!" A few times, unable to contain himself, the woodcock flew a song flight, only to be pursued in mid-air and escorted beyond the field. Once, a particularly aggressive bird collided with him at the apex of his flight, sending him reeling to the tree line.

By now he had given up finding a field of his own. Instead he flew a short distance from the pond to an open-

ing next to a road and waited for his chance. He witnessed from a safe and silent distance the dominant bird
mate with no fewer than four different hens over a period
of two weeks, sometimes copulating the same female
three times in a row.

One evening something peculiar happened. Two men
parked a truck on the road next to the field and stood as
if waiting for someone. The male began peenting at the
usual time, but the moment he lifted off the ground he
was stopped in mid-flight and floundered, suspended in
mid-air. The woodcock watched the men move quickly,
turn on a light, and pluck the bird out of the diffused
darkness. They walked back to the car, huddled briefly,
and a few minutes later released him. The woodcock
heard the car move down the road and watched until he
lost its lights. It was still early, but the other bird didn't
return.

The woodcock walked out of hiding and, after a moment's hesitation, began singing. Nothing drastic happened, so he flew. He flew higher and higher, in ever-
smaller ellipses, until hundreds of feet in the air he
hovered, chirped, and pitched down to earth, singing his
song over and over. Slipping sideways, he dived, checked
his fall, canted his wings and glided the remaining few

feet. At impact he whirled his feathers, stopped his momentum, and landed softly on his feet.

He flew three times. Between each peent he uttered a soft, gurgling "tuk-oo" under his breath. His last flight was rewarded. The hen had flown in quietly from the bordering cover while he was dancing and had walked the remaining distance. The woodcock fanned his tail, feigned alarm, and strutted over. He circled, raised his wings upright over his head, took a few more steps, dropped his wings so that they cupped his body, and inched forward. Not ready or willing, she moved off, and the woodcock sprang into flight. He landed twice more, attempting to mate, but each time she moved away. The third time he landed, she was gone.

He sang again at dawn, to no avail, then fed and rested in the alders, returning that evening, but the other bird was back and chased him away.

The life cycle of a woodcock originates on the singing grounds. The courtship, mating, spring diurnal and nocturnal cover, and to a certain extent nesting takes place either in or close to those grounds. As in so many of his ways, he is very specific about his needs but willing to compromise almost endlessly. Sonographic research, in conjunction with observation data, tells us that an average field contains one dominant male and 1.9 subdominant males. It is generally accepted that the dominant bird is older and returns to the same field year after year. The clearings may be anywhere from the size of a basketball court to as big as a football field, but there are prerequisites which make one more appealing than another. There should be groundcover in the form of grass and shrubbery, and it has been demonstrated that, up to a point, high shrub density improves the habitat, if only because it offers protection from predators. However, the urge to mate being what it is, the woodcock will often take what's available. Two-tracks and open pastures may not suit their whims, but they have been seen singing on both.

Ideally, the edges bordering the courtship area should not be too high. The bird begins his dance by flying low, and smaller trees surrounding the field give him an escape route if he needs it. Otherwise suitable fields are passed over because of high cover in the axis of possible flight patterns.

The quality of singing fields declines as the forest matures, much as does the bird's diurnal cover. In terms of decades, optimum habitat exists but briefly and shrinks rapidly as the hardwoods mature. It has been estimated that the annual loss of active sites throughout the United States is 3.3% per annum. Multiplied over a few decades this is a sizeable loss.

The woodcock romance is an odd one. On one hand, the male begins his saraband when the intensity of light is exactly 0.05 footcandles, or under normal conditions, twenty-two minutes after sunset. His romance lasts forty-five minutes, only to begin again at dawn when the light increases to the intensity of his last evening flight. On the other hand, woodcock have been heard peenting all night long, in parking lots and town squares. That the woodcock is an individual there is little doubt; that he is priapic there is less doubt; and that his charm lies in all that, as well as in his healthy appetite, makes him enviable.

The adjective "priapic" is used metaphorically. "Vent" is a better description of the male's accoutrement, and mating is a precarious affair. The male mounts the hen bird from behind, holding himself in position with a leg on her back and steadying himself by flailing his wings. She in turn twists her tail to one side so that both vents are brought together. One can easily imagine a certain amount of toppling over, reminiscent of the *comedies de boudoir* so favored by the French.

Eggs are puzzling. I love their shape and texture, and I enjoy eating them, but I don't understand how they harden and don't know how so many fit inside certain birds. Woodcock, for instance, hatch anywhere from two to six, six being an unusually high number, four being the average. They are pinkish-cinnamon in color and covered with small, irregular brown markings. Woodcock eggs are big, as big as grouse eggs, and weigh approximately 15 grams. If we estimate the spring weight of a female bird at 200 grams, her four eggs would weigh over a quarter as much as she does. I think of laborious running starts, ponderous landings, not to mention omelettes, but the fact is, hen woodcock lay one egg a day until the clutch is complete.

The information gathered from the banding of female woodcock and their broods is important. A nationwide program is conducted, partly realized by the FWS and

Departments of Natural Resources (DNR) and partly by volunteers, most of whom are hunters. Since the program began in 1959, approximately 50,000 woodcock have been banded. Unfortunately, the public appears to be running out of interest and the agencies out of money. Fewer and fewer birds are being tagged (2,573 birds in 1977, 1,187 in 1982, and 912 in 1983). The return of bands is low, about 3%, but even at that figure, they tell the story of a bird's migration, age, sex, breeding habitat, and a diversity of behavioral patterns.

Male woodcock, once they have mated, do not aid in rearing their progeny. Females incubate for twenty or twenty-one days, and during this time the hens are so reluctant to abandon their nests that some have uncharacteristically allowed themselves to be touched by man. The nest itself is rudimentary -- a slight depression in the ground, a few leaves and twigs to contour the shape of her body. The safety of the hen and her clutch lies in the bird's camouflage, her immobility, and the fact that while incubating she gives off very little scent. As with most shore birds, the eggs are pointed so that the smaller ends face toward the middle, taking up as little space as possible. The hen leaves her eggs to feed in the morning and again in the evening. Although a great many nests are found near singing grounds, the adjacent vegetation varies. They are often concealed by fallen branches, tree stumps and rotting logs. Natural sites are edges of clearings, bushy mounds, hummocks next to bogs, openings in conifer stands, and islands of second-growth trees, but characteristically, some nests are found in the middle of open fields and prairies where they normally shouldn't be.

The annual hatching time varies from thirty-six to forty-eight hours. While inside the egg the chick's neck and head are folded under its right wing. With the help of an "egg tooth" located on its upper mandible, the bird pips a hole through the rounded end of the egg and over a period of hours contracts its body and splits the shell lengthwise -- a unique procedure in that other birds split their eggs across. The false tooth falls off or disintegrates soon after hatching.

A newly hatched chick weighs an average of 12 grams. As soon as the egg moisture dries, the bird becomes active and is led away from the nest by its mother. The chicks more than likely feed on the egg white, are then to a certain extent fed by the mother, but within twenty-four hours are able to forage on their own. They probably rely on ants, larvae and bugs for the first few days, but worms become their staple diet the moment their bills are long enough and hard enough to probe with. The growth of hatchlings is phenomenal. In ten days the bird will weigh four times its birth weight and three weeks later will be indistinguishable from its mother.

* * *

I got in touch with David and Sally Downer in Traverse City. Sally had banded more woodcock than any other woman in Michigan in 1982, and it was over her setter, Ike, that I saw my first brood. I knew of Sally's father and uncle, Bill and Jack Wicksall. They were woodcock hunters whose reputation has grown over the years into legendary proportions. In 1971, while everyone else was arduously cutting swath through the woods looking for grouse, the Wicksall brothers concentrated on woodcock, kept their mouths shut, and enjoyed an extra decade of privacy. Raised in Europe, I found the general lack of interest in American woodcock hunting odd. Over there the bird is prized, and a few hundred acres of good cover in France might fetch ten thousand dollars a year for the hunting rights alone. Michigan inherited tens of thousands of public acres of the best woodcock habitat on the continent, but it wasn't until 1975 that my friends awakened to the fact that they were passing by a delicacy for the sake of tradition. Sally's uncle passed away in 1981, breaking up a thirty-year-old team, a team that had hunted as many as seven English setters at once, covering the fields like platoons of foxhounds. Because one member was right-handed and the other left-handed, the two men had walked in the forest on the same side of each other for two generations.

We were in the field by quarter of nine -- David, Sally, Ike and me. Ike was a two-year-old English setter whose pedigree went back to the original Wicksall dogs and whose mother, Ticker, was busily mothering a second litter of eight-day-old pups back at the house. Sally Downer is a tall, handsome woman, whose gentleness towards her dogs is touching. We were southeast of Traverse City, less than three hundred yards from where Jim, Nick and I had worked Nick's shorthair the previous day. We had flushed three males but had not found a single nest. We searched in deep cover, but Sally was working small, wooded islands surrounded by singing fields. We walked slowly, more slowly than we would if we were hunting, and Sally never took her eyes off her dog.

The reports had been poor, partly due to the harsh

spring weather that had followed the mild winter. To date Sally had been out three times and banded one brood next to her house, overlooking the Boardman River. We all felt that the season was late, and I worried, just as I do after a few empty hours of hunting, that I wasn't going to see what I came for. Ike did his job well, covering the ground quickly without ranging. The Wicksalls had bred their dogs with grouse and woodcock in mind, intending the dogs to be small and close-working. They had accomplished both.

Ike tightened up on the edge of a poplar patch next to a single jack pine. Sally gestured for us to stop and, quietly "whoaing" Ike, stared at the ground. I looked hard at the area close to the setter and beyond but didn't see a thing. Sun-speckled tapestries left over from fall carpeted the ground in puzzling uniformity.

David spotted the hen first. She sat facing away from us, flattened against the ground, her bill resting on the leaves and her black eyes looking straight ahead. No more than fifteen feet away, I had missed her a dozen times. She, on the other hand, could see us perfectly. In twelve years of hunting I had never seen a bird other than in flight, except once for a fraction of a second before it flushed. This bird was so still it was as though she weren't breathing. Sally became very feminine. She worried about the chicks and wouldn't let us move for fear of stepping on one. It took quite a while before we found them, immobile, a few yards from their mother. Once we had all four located, Sally tied Ike to a tree and prepared her banding equipment. When she was ready, David unfurled the nine-foot-long net he had been carrying and, mindful of the chicks, approached the hen, furtively raising the net above her in a smooth, slow-motion play that didn't work. At the last moment, with the net hovering a foot above her head, she flushed low under it, gained a little altitude, dropped her tail and legs and pretended to fall. Tipping and turning above the ground, she finally landed awkwardly in the grass twenty yards away. Everything I had read about the decoying act of a female woodcock was true.

Sally turned her attention to the chicks and, with the utmost gentleness, picked them up one by one and placed them in a small mesh bag. The first one peeped in a high falsetto voice, waking the others who then scrambled about on the ground. They were as delicate as meringue topping. Covered in thick buff down, mottled in varying shades of slate grey, they looked at us out of big, black eyes. Completely disproportioned, their bills were tiny and their feet huge. Sally removed four bands from the holding ring, took out a pair of surgical pliers and pried them open. She then readied her notebook and a short ruler. One by one David handed her the chicks, and she measured the length of their bills, noting in millimeters each one. The rule for aging hatchlings is the following: A chick is born with a fourteen-millimeter beak. The rate of growth per day is two millimeters, and therefore their age is tabulated by measuring the bill from the base of the skull to the tip, subtracting fourteen from that number, and dividing by two. In the case of our chicks, whose bills were twenty-two millimeters long, the equation made them four days old. This rule applies to bill lengths up to forty-five millimeters; after that the growth rate is irregular and cannot be computed.

Sally held the little birds as only a woman would. Had she been holding an egg, her breath would have warmed the yolk. The birds peeped, and she cooed back, obviously in a world that David and I knew nothing about. One by one she slipped the bands on their grown-up legs, tightened them with her surgical pliers, making sure the ends didn't overlap, and placed them under my hat on the ground. When all four birds were banded, Sally made a few notes, asked David to move Ike away from

the brood, picked up the net and her kit and, walking a few feet away, asked me to raise the hat. The four chicks were balled up together, looking serenely at me. They never moved an inch.

It was a fine performance and executed with consideration for a world that more than likely will not exist a century from now. Sally was flushed and maternal. I didn't know at the time that she was expecting a child of her own.

We hunted Ike unsuccessfully for another hour. High clouds covered the sun, and a misty rain shortened the search. Two blue racers startled me on the way back to the car. Entwined on the ground, they looked like an Egyptian staff. Back at the house I played with the pups and met Sally's father. He sat in what was obviously his chair and told me of hunts that he and his brother had made before I was born. With memories to spare, his eyes glowed softly in the recesses of the past. He and Sally would hunt together that fall and would walk slowly side by side, led by her setters: an aged man and his only daughter.

That evening a friend of Jim's dropped off two dozen white wing doves, shot earlier that year in Mexico. Jim Harrison's affection for game is common knowledge in the county, and partly as a form of remuneration for his art and partly in the hope of being invited to hunt, friends and acquaintances bestow on him gifts of wild foods.

Dusk usually finds the Harrison household in a fever of activity, and the promise of game only intensified the situation. We decided the birds would be cooked on the grill, and Nick Reens was called in as the expert in that field. Wine, butter, potatoes and vegetables were readied under the watchful eyes of two Laboradors, a young Airedale bitch, two cats and Jim's younger daughter, Anna, who by and by tired of waiting and settled for a grilled cheese in front of the television. Nick arrived, actively massaging his beard in a familiar gesture of anticipation, and handed over a warm, road-killed woodcock to add to the pot. When no one was watching, I hid it in the icebox. It would be consumed, but not three hours after four-day-old nestlings had stared into my eyes.

Woodcock prefer worms to any other food, and much like the group of gluttons working the kitchen that night, they eat great quantities. Captive woodcock have been known to eat their own weight (150 grams) of lumbricidae in a twenty-four-hour-period, and it is logical to assume that, given the chance, they would do so in the wild. Exclusive of worms, woodcock, eat other invertebrates such as ants, beetle larvae, snails, caterpillars, flies, an occasional moth caught on the wing, as well as small amounts of vegetable matter. Corn, raspberries, alder leaves, ragweed, and other matter surface during dissections, but cannot be thought of as the bird's staple diet. It is more likely that they are incidentally ingested during periods of inclement weather or simply because it happened to be attached to the invertebrates consumed. The reason woodcock eat such a large quantity of worms is because earthworms are mostly made of water (85%) and yield a very low dry-weight biomass. It comes down to the correlation of energy needed to collect food and energy in the form of protein acquired and stored for the bird's sustenance. In the case of worms the net protein gain is very low and explains the need for quantity. Undoubtedly the bird would be better off if its diet were geared towards secondary preferences, since larvae, beetles and such contain more protein in relation to their weight, but for reasons known only to the woodcock, his gastronomic life cycle is focused.

This was probably not always the case. Ten thousand years ago, when the northern part of the continent was frozen, there were no earthworms. In fact, between that time and the colonization of the States in the seventeenth and eighteenth centuries, it is believed that there were no indigenous worms inhabiting the northern summer grounds of woodcock. Basically, they were introduced in the East via Europe and in the West by way of Asia. The carriers were probably imported potted plants, dear to the wives of the colonists. One might assume that without worms the birds would have restricted their range to the southern half of the country, but a 1634 report of Iroquois Indians eating woodcock in Quebec suggests that the birds had adapted their diet instead.

There is an obvious correlation between the habitat of woodcock and earthworm profusion. When soil samples are tested for acidity, temperature, moisture, nitrogen content and worm population (ingeniously measured by permeating quadrants of earth with a solution of formaldehyde and collecting the worms that surface), the surveys demonstrate that the highest counts of worms are obtained in areas of alders and aspens, which are also prime woodcock cover. In time of drought, a higher percentage of worms and birds are found in conifer stands, not a preferred cover but one that offers more shade and therefore less moisture loss.

Nineteenth-century observers describing woodcock foraging for food maintained that the birds bored holes in the earth and then beat the ground with either their wings or bills, luring the curious worms from the ready-made openings. A report in the *American Turf Register*, dated February, 1830, describes a woodcock feeding by impaling his bill in the ground, raising himself off his feet, opening his wings, fanning his tail, and pirouetting on his beak until it was sufficiently embedded to reach his prey. A little in the varied and comic manner of humans, woodcock feeding habits vary, from the stealthy ear-to-the-ground approach, to the incisive parry-and-thrust method, to the bobbing and weaving stalk reminiscent of reggae dancers. It would be interesting to observe the stand-off between a woodcock and a large Alabama fighting worm. It might give a simple-minded producer an idea for a movie script.

* * *

There are different ways of walking through the woods. The correct method should look effortless and becomes so with practice. In fact, it is matter of angles, like poling a skiff or paddling a canoe. It is mostly anticipation, unwasted motion, being pliant to resistance and comfortable under pressure. Bob Odom walks that way and never loses his hat.

Jim and I met him at the DNR office in Traverse City, an hour or so after he had qualified for the volunteer fire force by running a mile and a half in under eleven minutes. A long-legged man in his thirties, Odom has worked out of Traverse City for seven years and is Michigan's best woodcock bander. I should have suspected something when I noticed his ragged briar-proof hunting pants. Harrison and I were dressed for a stroll, and it turned out to be just that, except that it was performed at high speed and lasted four and a half hours.

Odom had banded a hundred and forty-three birds the previous year, exactly one hundred more than Sally Downer, and I suspect that at least one reason for his success is that he covers three times as much ground. He owns two setters, a big-going, square-headed male named Petey Boy and a small, close-working bitch named Daisy. The dogs complement each other, and as is the case with some dog handlers, Bob doesn't own a whistle and doesn't raise his voice. He does, however, tie a strip of highly visible Day-glo surveyors' tape to their collars.

We started next to a creek bottom Jim and I had

hunted for years, and as hunters do when they meet for the first time, we didn't elaborate on each other's knowledge of cover. By the end of the day we knew that we had all hunted each other's territories, and we were at ease comparing notes. We kept some secrets, but such is the way of upland bird-hunters.

We found our first brood quickly, and Bob netted the female, followed by the chicks. Two things struck me: neither dog had to be tied while we were banding, and Bob was very quick about his business. Although he held the hen, and later the chicks, gently in his hand, he was accurate and very precise about gathering the data and getting the birds back on the ground. All the while, Daisy crept closer and closer on her belly until her nose was an inch from the hatchlings. A look of bewildered curiosity wrinkled her eyes, and her nose twitched, but she never made a sudden move. The chicks were so delicate, I felt like lying in the grass and letting them run up and down my chest. Something about them made me think of dandelions.

For the first hour or so we worked softer cover than I had with Sally. Standing puddles reflected images of clouds, and the footing was precarious. Bob finds broods every year so close to water that some nests lie on tiny islands the size of bedside tables. As a rule, though, nesting sites are covered with leaves and needles, with some grass underfoot. They lie next to low shrubs, seedlings or slash, and close to edges of second-growth hardwoods. But then, rules don't always apply.

Nothing is better for hunting dogs than spring banding. It gets them back into a semblance of shape, and more important it teaches them to be staunch on point. Bob's were a pleasure to follow. Petey's casts were long and loping, while Daisy worked circles within a perimeter of twenty yards. Over a given year, they find an equal number of birds.

Green stains of wild leeks sprouted next to a solitary oak, and I plucked a handful. They tasted like a hybrid garlic. We looked for morels but were too early. They needed a rain and a warm, sunny day. Odom mentioned that Andy Ammann equates mushrooms and nesting sites, both being whimsical and unpredictable.

The name most mentioned in the world of woodcock, particularly when it comes to banding, is Andy Ammann. He might be thought of as the dean of woodcock. Over the years he has devoted himself to their well-being and pursuit, both with tags and guns. An older gentleman, Ammann considers himself basically a lover and observer of nature. Most recent innovations in the capture and identification of woodcock have come from his inquisitive and resourceful mind, such as the system, which he developed from an older method, for aging woodcock eggs by suspending them in water. The closer the eggs are to hatching, the less they weigh and the higher they float -- not recommended practice for amateurs, who might unwillingly prompt the hen to abandon her nest, but necessary to those professionals who need to know when to return.

We walked and talked for a long time before finding another brood. The weather was good and the woods full of spring activity. A heavy log covered with fresh droppings pinpointed an earlier sound of drumming, and deer scattered, bounding in front of the dogs. Grouse flushed, sometimes wild and sometimes following roading points. Male woodcock kept us guessing, and an occasional skein of ducks punctured the sky. The air was fresh and dried our perspiration. From time to time Bob would point out good nesting sites, but I couldn't pick out a pattern or see that any one spot was better than another. I believe he was speaking from experience, but maybe it was more the sixth sense that woodsmen acquire after a decade or so in the field.

Odom hadn't noticed much of a decline in the woodcock population over the years, but he had noticed that
the hunters had multiplied. On the Eastern Seaboard,
habitat loss is the main reason for the steady decline of
birds. It is not as much of a factor in Michigan.
Granted, a few singing fields are turned into shopping
centers, and every year more land is posted, but overall
northern Michigan is a huge wilderness, comparatively
safe for the years to come. All one has to do is look at
the map and glance to the Upper Peninsula. One gets
the idea that bears and wolves still roam the forests, and
so they do. Michigan woodcock have a lot of leeway in
their search for privacy, and many will never see a
human in their lifetime. Hunting pressure is a fact to
contend with, but for the moment it seems to be localized, and when one studies the flush-per-hour ratios of
woodcock hunters, one is reassured that most don't have
the slightest idea where to go, what to look for, or what
to do if they get there.

Insofar as woodcock management is concerned, Odom
feels that there is little that can be done by the state. Rye
fields planted by the DNR to help deer through the
winters are used by woodcock as singing fields. The
agency works with lumber companies so that specific cut-

tings are made to benefit game, but other than that, the bird is very much on its own.

We banded two more broods before the day's end, saw a total of six male woodcock, and flushed seven grouse. Bob was disappointed. The track we had worked should have produced more broods, but he felt we were early. Checking out previous data, he placed optimum hatching time at May tenth and insisted that most amateurs look for the birds too early in the season and get discouraged before the time is right.

We followed Bob back to his house, where his son was nurturing a young badger. The boy and the badger seemed on good terms. Bob had to prepare himself for a meeting and later was going to walk a three-mile survey route for singing birds. Jim and I stopped off at Sleder's Bar, had a couple, and, feeling our aches, mused about getting into shape.

* * *

I awoke on May eighth in a snowstorm in North Bay, Ontario. I had driven through rain all the way from Jim's to Sault Ste. Marie and along the north shore of Lake Huron. By midnight the rain had crystallized and in the morning was a foot thick on the car. It was,

nevertheless, a beautiful drive, and the marriage of conifers and dark lakes reminded me of the Black Forest of Germany. The food in Ontario is not the same as in Quebec, influenced, in fact, by two unnoteworthy cuisines, English and North American Midwest. My ennui reflected both styles of cooking; on the other hand, it had been served by a young and pretty moon-faced Indian girl with a slightly awkward walk.

The following night I stayed in the town of Rivière du Loup, for no other reason than I liked its name. The next day it misted the whole way down to Calais, but for some reason it fit the landscape.

My drive east coincided with the northernmost range of two of the three woodcock flyways. These flyways are recognized as the Atlantic, Central and Western, but in reality they overlap. In theory, birds that breed in the Maritime Provinces follow the Eastern Seaboard as far as Cape May, New Jersey, where the flights either branch off in a westerly course across the Appalachian Mountains to the Mississippi Delta or continue south through the Carolinas, Alabama and northern Florida. The Central flyway originates anywhere from the middle section of Quebec, western Ontario or Michigan and sweeps south, meeting somewhere in Tennessee before continuing down to Mississippi and Louisiana. Finally, the Western flyway begins either in Wisconsin or Minnesota and takes a direct route down the Mississippi River to Louisiana and eastern Texas.

The distribution of woodcock through the eastern half of the United States is complex. Some birds do not migrate north in the spring but nest on their wintering grounds; others, in times of clement weather, winter as far north as Pennsylvania. There have been reports, substantiated and otherwise, of woodcock in Bermuda, as far west as the city of Los Angeles, and south to Martinique. (The last seems doubtful, as the sighting was made a century ago by a local dandy leaving a bar at sunup.) Birds banded as chicks in South Carolina and Alabama have been shot the same fall in Michigan, and birds banded in eastern Michigan have been found in western Minnesota, which means the migration of the Carolina and Alabama birds took place in the late spring or summer, not a usual occurrence. The second report would indicate that woodcock move freely from east to west and back, as well as north and south. I believe the migration is twofold: some birds hold to a pattern, while others, more daring, wander in search of different horizons. Of course, to a great extent these wanderings are affected by wind, and certainly weather motivates the occasional bird that visits Bermuda.

From 1972 to 1974 an experiment was made to establish the bird in California. Up until then sightings of woodcock west of the Continental Divide were rare and mostly unsubstantiated. The point of the experiment was to establish a wintering ground for woodcock in the Sacramento Valley in the hope that a northerly migration from there up to Oregon and Canada would occur. Over a two-year period, a total of 599 woodcock were trapped in Louisiana, crated and airshipped to San Francisco. The results were minimal. A handful returned to Louisiana, while one bird was sighted 120 miles northeast of Anchorage, Alaska, another in Kansas, and a third near Ely, Nevada. The Nevada bird would have had to have flown across hundreds of miles of desert and at times as high as 8000 feet. Finally, a bird bearing the band of the California experiment was shot on September 30, 1974, outside St. Ignace, Michigan. He is referred to as the "Mackinac Bridge Woodcock," and his travels were as daring as Pegasus' attempt at the heavens. The experiment was aborted in 1975.

Woodcock have been seen in the streets of New York City, sharing chicken coops in Kansas, perched on the branches of trees, and swimming across water holes on golf courses. One was captured in 1949 strutting down the runway of the aircraft carrier U.S.S. Midway, eighty-two miles south of Nantucket Island. Others have been observed chasing hawks from singing grounds. The bird is a master of the unpredictable and behaves like a hobo. His abnormal migration is in fact normal for him.

* * *

Calais, Maine, is a little border town on the edge of the St. Croix River. The houses are large, white, and topped with steep-shingled roofs. Heating is a seasonal problem, and the people of Calais, noted for their frugality, look at them in terms of wood: "That thar house is a fifteen-cord one for sure!"

God-fearing and proud by nature, the people of Calais are mostly comprised of lumbermen and fishermen. They do not like Calais to be pronounced any way but "Calase" and resent the fact that Canadians articulate it in the French manner. Except for Cook's Inlet in Alaska, the St. Croix River's twenty-eight-foot tides are the highest in the continental United States.

Florida license plates and dark-tinted windows incited a U.S. Customs agent to a thorough inquisition. After computerizing my passport, the bald, slow-speaking officer read every one of my notes, including official letters from the Department of the Interior, and then, with a gleam in his eye, took to my car. My suggestion that he body-search the dog cost me an extra forty-five minutes in the government parking lot. By and by, he steered me to a motel, and when questioned about food he grudgingly admitted that a couple of New Yorkers had recently opened a restaurant but added, "Thar food's too fancy for me."

The Moosehorn National Wildlife Refuge, four miles south of Calais, was founded in 1937 and is primarily geared to the study of woodcock. The sixteen thousand acres in one section and sixty-five hundred a few miles away were repossessed by the government after a series of fires destroyed the forest and small farms of the area. Forty-five years later the fauna is mostly second-growth stands and a handful of surviving white pines. Two small lakes, fifty flowages, bogs and marshes, abandoned farms, and rocky shorelines bordering the St. Croix River make this refuge a perfect habitat for North American mammals from shrews and harbor seals to bear and moose. The estimated summer waterfowl population stands at eighteen hundred, the woodcock at eleven hundred with an additional fifteen hundred during the fall.

The head biologist at Moosehorn is Greg Sepik, a bright, slightly built man sporting a fair beard beneath piercing blue eyes. I found out quickly that he would answer any and all questions as long as they were thoughtfully phrased; otherwise, he would stare into the middle distance and wait until they were. My father was a scientist, and I was familiar with this. Conjecture is one thing, but hard facts constitute a jubilee.

The study of *Scolopax minor* grudgingly surrenders hard facts. It is a problem of numbers. Even at Moosehorn, where work is conducted from spring through mid-fall with added help from college students in the summer, the few hundred birds collected, banded and studied are but an asterisk in the computer. I have read a great many papers written by eminent biologists who used fewer than a dozen birds for their data, and I have been struck by the confidence of their assumptions. During the two days I spent at the Moosehorn Refuge, however, Greg underplayed his role, qualified his answers, referred some questions to the future, and passed others on to men he considered more knowledgeable than himself.

Most of my queries directed at this man with a degree in biology were inane, but Greg was gracious and at worst noncommital. When I inquired about pesticides, he replied that since the banning of DDT he didn't see them as a major problem. For the most part 2-4-5T with Dioxin is sprayed at worst every forty years on any given acre of land in Maine and New Brunswick. The bird wings sampled at Patuxent for residue do not indicate cause for alarm. I was disappointed, not because I wanted the birds to be tainted, but because chemical spraying is something I understand but detest. Certainly, one may conjecture that the accumulation of substances such as chlorinated naphthllene and phosphates, ingested via game birds and stored in our bodies over a period of years, will surface in the form of melanomas, mutations, or simply in psychological disorders.

Greg's work is varied, but his goal is results. The most concrete work done to date at Moosehorn is in land management. Over the years new singing fields have been carved out of the forests by means of clearcutting, salvage cutting, and burning, in an effort to change the existing habitat. Prior to this work the most common sites for singing grounds in the area were blueberry fields, but the birds rarely use them any more. The attempt is to manipulate the land and offer woodcock the correct vegetable and structural composition, while leaving slash cover as a protection from predators. Sepik told me the experiment lured males immediately and prompted an invasion of females two years later. Since then woodcock abundance has quadrupled in the managed areas.

Greg's goal is to educate landowners in methods that will help game proliferate. To date, many assume that untended land is better suited to game. They are mistaken. Deer, grouse and woodcock do not like climax forests. Greg feels that with the help of aerial maps and forestry advisors, landowners can improve habitat by cutting openings in the hardwoods, as well as clear-cutting areas of alders and balsam. The new growths provide cover for grouse and woodcock, browse for deer, and in most cases allow the landowner to collect from the sale of the timber.

We took a tour of the refuge, and Greg pointed out the work in progress. The man-made fields ranged from ten acres in size down to an acre or less. Flags of tape on surveyor stakes fluttered in the wind, and I was told that in the summer, when his students collect and band birds at night, they get so turned around that they use the stakes as reference points. Shining is done with powerful quartz iodine racing car lights, powered by motorcycle batteries. The birds are disoriented and either captured on the ground or flushed and followed until they land, at which point they are culled with a long-handled net. The best weather is an overcast night, preferably with a light rain. There must be no fog and no visible horizon, as the light will not penetrate the former and woodcock fly to the latter. In a light rain, with no horizon to orient to, the birds flush and alight quickly. On good nights the students band approximately twenty woodcock. The record is forty-seven, collected in a downpour between ten p.m. and daybreak.

Sepik also uses mist nets and traplines. The nets are used during the courtship period and in the summer to capture woodcock coming into the fields to roost, while the traplines, which work on the principle of weirs, can be used any time. The traps are set in good daytime cover, and when the birds bump into them, instead of flying they follow the wire mesh until they find themselves inside the cage. Decoy traps were also used on singing fields in the past, and in certain areas they still are. Decoys lure males by presenting them with a stuffed counterpart. The males have been known to copulate with the decoys, sometimes as often as two and three times in a row. Shameless, they don't seem to mind one-sided adventures.

Our first night out was clear and bitterly cold. A couple from Pennsylvania who had driven up to Maine to observe harbor seals joined us, along with Greg's two daughters, Molly, eight years old, and Emily, age three. The nets were already in place next to the road adjoining a two-acre field, and they had only to be unfurled. Made in Japan, they are thirty feet long and ten feet high. The point is to intercept a singing bird either when he lifts into flight or when he returns, so the nets are raised off the ground and strategically placed in accordance with flight patterns. Sometimes it doesn't work, though, and that night was one of those times. I played with the girls, who both wore buttercup smiles and whose mother, I was told, was finishing her last year in Pittsburgh before becoming a certified nurse. I also stomped around a lot, trying to keep warm. Greg takes his girls on all his night hunts.

The woodcock sang but eluded the net. The couple from Pennsylvania never saw him, even though he was outlined time after time in the sky, but then they hadn't seen the harbor seals, either.

At the restaurant I ordered a double dry martini and whimsically envied Greg's knowledge of forestry and wildlife. It had been refreshing talking to a person who volunteered information because he cared. Next to me, a table of real estate persons discussed credit cards and the banality of prime rates. Across the room the local IGA owner ate holding his fork in his fist and paid his bill from a stack of hundreds that bulged his hip pocket. After my lobster, the owner joined me in a brandy and described the moose he and his son had poached that winter.

Greg had done telemetry work with woodcock before and was gearing up for a full summer's worth of it. He felt that this intensified study would open the doors to many unanswered questions about habitat preference, diurnal and nocturnal movements, behavior of incubating hens, causes of mortality, post-migratory grouping of birds, behavior of yearlings, and dates of migrations. The radio transmitters weigh 5 grams and are glued and strapped onto the birds' backs in a way that doesn't hinder flight. The reception and monitoring is done by summer students and the data fed into Greg's computer. The scene made me think of the arcade-like quality of the control room at NASA headquarters.

One of the problems with the scientific process is the time lapse between field work and published results, a process which takes years. Worse perhaps is the fact that the results rarely get into the hands of the public. When I stopped in Laurel, Maryland, at the Patuxent Research Station, which is the national headquarters for all North American migratory birds, I could not believe the vast amount of research performed and how little the layman hears of it. It was explained to me that if a particular branch of the Department of the Interior makes public too much information, citizens might insist on more funding and put unwanted pressure on Congress. Departments are therefore advised to do their work and keep the results within the community, another example of conducting business at public expense and at the expense of men and women who labor hard only to see their work shelved.

The second night Greg took his daughters and me to a different location. We drove past some of the fifty flowages on the refuge, stopping every time so that the girls could watch the geese. Molly remembered the exact spot she had seen a bear, but we didn't discuss it too much because Emily was still a little unsure about bears. We had a little time after setting up, and I played Pooh

Sticks with the girls. Greg told me that the oldest woodcock recaptured at the refuge was at least nine years old. Emily wanted to know what we were going to catch, and I replied, "A cow." She was puzzled but liked the idea.

We saw the bird fly into his field, and in the next few minutes I counted five more flying to their respective clearings, but once again we were unlucky. The bird flew and flew but missed the net every time. Greg peented and was rewarded with the birds cacking back and flying at his face. He ran into the field while the woodcock was airborne and tried flushing it into the net, but all we caught was a starling. It didn't matter. The procedure was obvious, the night air crowded with distant mating calls, and the little girls full of mischief. Before we left, Emily placed her hands on her hips and, looking up at her father, inquired: "Daddy, where's the cow?"

That evening I was lonely and caught a condition the French call *vin triste* ("sad wine"). I returned to my motel room, packed, and told my dog that we were in the wrong line of work. Her eyes were like dark pats of butter and radiated a lifetime of trust. How could she know that someday she would be too old to hunt and that soon after she would die? All she knew was that she loved me and that together we had nudged dun-colored skies into fanfares of wings, whimpered and cut ourselves on talus faces, lost ourselves in sweltering bogs, and found birds where there should have been none. We understood each other better than most men understand God. More important, we hoped that when autumn came, the birds would fly.

The woodcock was a year old. He had made it while most of his peers had not. Perhaps he would grow to be nine years old like that other bird and over his lifetime fly some twenty thousand miles across the land, but meanwhile something was happening. He was gradually losing the desire to dance. Food was more interesting, and his visits to the fields no longer held priority. The weather was warming, and the buds on the trees had turned to leaves. He knew that he had missed something but couldn't remember exactly what.

TWO

The nights are brief, midday visions diffused, and the perpendicular quest for energy has finally altered sap to chlorophyll. It is summer, and nature suggests the illusion of immortality.

The broods have dispersed, and for some, as in the case of the North Carolina hatchling recovered in Michigan, summer is a time for adventure. For others, the general vicinity of their birthplace remains home. The fledglings test their instincts, and the mature birds pursue the daily routine of probing for worms. A percentage of the yearlings have died, but the rest command an ever-increasing chance of living.

Mature woodcock begin the summer underweight, the males from singing and fretting and the females from tending to their young. Droughts produce disasters. The worms estivate and are unreachable. Moisture is imperative to the birds' survival.

Woodcock fare poorly under abstinence. In tests, captive birds fed a minimal 20 grams of earthworms a day died in forty-eight hours, having lost 40% of their body weight. Woodcock can live for a period of time on 60 grams of worms a day but generally lose 30% of their body mass and die after a two-week period. During the summer months the birds seek the moisture of stream bottoms and alder thickets. In periods of great heat, they quite often rest under the shade of conifers.

A great deal has been written on the evening flights of woodcock to open fields, and for a long time those flights were believed to be prompted by strict feeding habits. Even though most of the literature cites these nocturnal migrations, foraging is not always the primary motivation and in fact may not be a reason at all. Professor Keith Causey of Auburn University responded to my inquiry:

... There are many reasons why woodcock might elect to roost in openings, including avoidance of predation, or as a means of daily exercise, a routine to keep flight muscles fit for upcoming migratory journeys.

Woodcock, like most creatures, have a programmed circadian rhythm. Dawn and dusk flights are a part of this daily activity pattern. They also feed heavily at dawn and dusk and this would be the case whether they were in forests or fields at these times.

... The bottom line seems to be that many woodcock roost in openings of varying sizes. They do some feeding after they arrive and to some degree during the course of

the night. The purpose for this behavior (using openings at night) is not presently known and could be for a variety of reasons that may change from time to time or place to place.

The traditional naturalistic assumption that woodcock go to night fields in order to feed is an unsupported speculation.

Interestingly enough, birds do use certain fields on summer nights and in some cases *en masse.* Perhaps this behavior is linked to the woodcock's genetic background: shore birds are communal by nature. In the days of market hunters, anywhere from one to two thousand woodcock were shipped weekly to the New York market every summer, and most had been shot at night. Nowadays, if the conditions are right, the most effective means of collecting woodcock is still by shining. It is also a fact that a high percentage of birds captured in the summer fields are young males and that those same fields were predominantly those used in the spring for mating.

Summer flights also include a certain amount of practice courtship. Young males have been heard peenting and singing at dusk as if gearing up for the following year. The intensity is not the same, and there can be more than one bird performing in a given field, but like all young males they appear to be flexing their egos in anticipation of things to come.

Summer represents a resting time for woodcock. Other than feeding and later molting, the bird's activities are relatively sedate, offering us here a timely disgression into a look at *Scolopax minor's* relatives and a few historical anecdotes.

The European woodcock and the owl were religious symbols, allegorically representing meditation and the solitary staff. A seventeenth-century calendar printed in Brittany depicts Christ on a cross, at the bottom of which a coiled snake is being struck in the head by a woodcock. The Spanish named her (in Europe most everything of beauty is thought of in the feminine) *la ciega,* the blind hen. The Germans say *Schepfe,* which means beak. The French called her *bécade* and later *bécasse,* which translates to post. In Greek she is *Scolopax* because her beak resembles a stake and also a *Xylornitha,* which means a bird of the woods. In Latin she is a vagabond hen, a *Gallinago,* or again a sylvan partridge, a *Perdrix rusticola.* Her scientific name combines both Greek and Latin: *Scolopax rusticola.*

The most noticeable difference between the European and the American birds rests in their sizes. In hand,

Scolopax rusticola feels twice as heavy as our bird but actually averages somewhere between eleven and thirteen ounces, with a few individuals topping the pound. The heaviest bird ever reported was shot in Norfolk, England, in 1775 and weighed 835 grams, or twenty-seven ounces.

The bird's markings differ in many ways, but as the European bird varies in weight and coloring within the species and its range, the differences are subtle. Most notable is that the undercarriage of *Scolopax rusticola* is barred instead of uniformly colored, and that instead of four lateral bars across her forehead she usually bears three. The primary feathers are wider than those of *Scolopax minor* and do not vary between male and female, making external identification impossible.

The distribution of woodcock in Europe is extensive and in fact transcends to Asia Minor, east as far as Japan, and south to Malaysia. In the West the bird ranges from the Soviet Union (some feel that this is the original home of most European woodcock), Norway, Sweden and Finland in the north and spreads like an out-stretched hand down the Euro-Asiatic continent as far south as Morocco's Atlas range, to the Nile Valley and throughout all of North Africa. Pockets of birds are

found as far south as the Canary Islands, west to the Azores, and east to Japan, where they migrate north and south from the Japanese Alps down to the islands of Riuku, joining a subspecies known as *Scolopax rusticola mira.*

The migratory paths of *Scolopax rusticola* resemble a huge seine, roughly thrown across the middle of the Soviet Union from the northeast to west-southwest. From there the birds drain south. Woodcock are reported in Iran, Sri Lanka, and occasionally as far as Taima, Saudi Arabia. The Malaysian birds are for the most part sub-species and are believed to have migrated thousands of years ago from Burma and Thailand down as far as New Guina. In Djawa, the bird is known as *Scolopax saturata saturata* and is a smaller woodcock bearing a longer beak. In Sulawesi (the Celebes Islands) there are two subspecies, *Scolopax celebensis Heinrichi* and *Scolopax celebensis celebensis.* Finally, in New Guinea the bird is referred to as *Scolopax saturata Resenbergii* and is considered a delicacy by the Papou headhunters.

European birds that on rare occasions appear in North America are believed to have flown in from Iceland or from the Azores, but the sightings of *rusticola* on this side of the Atlantic are few, prompted by tremendous westerly winds in mid-ocean.

The yearly kill of woodcock in Europe is estimated at five to six million. When I first read that the French killed two million birds a season, I attributed the number to enthusiasm and legendary story-telling, but in fact the figures are correct. Running a close second and third are Italy and Russia, with yearly kills of a million and a half birds. Great Britian, where much of the history of superlative woodcock hunting originates, is fourth with a kill of two hundred thousand birds. The mathematics of the situation are obvious: four or five countries kill 90% of the bag. To put things in perspective, the French kill as many woodcock as are killed in the entire United States.

Basically, the life expectancy, behavior and feeding habits of *Scolopax rusticola* are similar to those of *Scolopax minor,* but evolution and adaption to habitat find the European bird content to live deeper in the forests and in some regions in the conifers. *Scolopax rusticola* runs more than our bird, both while hunted as well as under normal daily conditions, and is known to jump over logs and debris up to two feet high. As these birds migrate considerably longer distances than do

North American woodcock, their mortality rate is higher. In times of adverse weather, reports of birds floundering by the thousands in the Baltic Sea are common. The oldest woodcock of any variety was a bird from Czechoslovakia, banded on June 17, 1935, and shot twenty-one years later on March 25, 1956.

The European bird does not sing but rather "rodes." During the courting period, the males fly above the treetops at dusk, emitting croaking noises to attract the females, who in turn call them back to the ground. Copulation is similar to that of the American woodcock. The nest, eggs and rearing of the young are also similar, with one exception: in times of danger the European woodcock carries her young for distances of a hundred yards or more.

The controversy surrounding hens flying chicks to safety is so old that I have seen seventeenth-century prints depicting the act. In Europe it is considered a *fait accompli,* and every book and hunter will attest to its authenticity. Most believe that the chicks are held between the mother's thighs, but some insist that they are clutched in the hen's feet, while still others describe the young being carried on her back. The latter methods are not probable. Logical reasoning implies that the airlift is accidental, the chicks happening to be in the right place when the hen flushed, but too many sightings of birds carrying one chick only to return and carry off a second and third have been made not to believe that the occurrence is true. *Scolopax minor* is also reputed to carry her young, but supposedly less frequently than her European counterpart. I have interviewed a great many people who work in the field for a living, as well as banders, birdwatchers and hunters. With one exception, no one has ever witnessed this phenomenon. The exception proving the rule is my friend, Dr. James Hall from Traverse City, Michigan, who observed a chick being carried by its mother. Dr. Hall is an excellent woodsman and a gentleman with impeccable credentials. If he saw it, it happened.

Another phenomenon no less puzzling came to my attention early one morning when a friend with a somewhat sooty sense of humor barked into the phone, "Heard about the short-billed woodcock?" Convinced he would parlay the question into something personal, I refused to buy it and hung up. A month later he sent me a small excerpt from *The Field*, a magazine published in England, in which an eminent biologist discussed the issue. A letter to Dr. John Harradine, research coordinator for the British Association for Shooting and Conservation, verified the fact that over a hundred short-billed woodcock have been recorded since 1948, including one return of seven short-billed birds shot in Calvados, France, on November 20, 1978. For all intents and purposes, the birds are identical to the common species, both in coloration and weight, except that their bills are one-third shorter. Dr. D. Fraguglione, who has done extensive research in France on the subject and who has tested short-billed woodcock for physical damage, biocides and chemical agents as well as radio-activity and the possibility that the birds were a hitherto-unknown subspecies, tentatively concludes that *Scolopax rusticola* is undergoing a genetic mutation, an evolutionary change related to its habitat and feeding habits. A call to the Migratory Research Center in Laurel, Maryland, indicates that there are, to date, no reports of short-billed woodcock in this country.

Up until a few years ago, Europe boasted long woodcock seasons and a variety of hunting methods. Driven shoots were common and deadly, particularly when they coincided with migrations. Shooting during the dusk flight was murderous, and during the spring roding season more so. Although the latter two methods have been abolished in most European countries, it was argued that the roding season killed predominantly the surplus males and in no way altered the following season's bag. In the past few years, gamekeepers and tenants alike agree that it did, if for no other reason than that it disrupted the mating cycle.

Reports a century old of drives in England, Scotland and Ireland, during which it was routine to bag a hundred woodcock a day, abound. One particular shoot as recent as 1937 relates that during a period of two weeks, hunting a five-day week, four guns shooting an estate in Argyll bagged 1,084 birds. A hundred years ago it was common in both France and Italy for a hunter to kill fifty birds a day, but the performance in 1831 by a Mr. B. of Framingham, England, that saw him single-handedly kill and bag, in heavy cover, one hundred and nine woodcock during a day's shooting, is the highest I have found. It is said that he used one hundred and eleven shells to perform the task.

Overall, there are no limits in Europe, a fact that explains why in France and Italy there are no indigenous game birds left. In Alphonse Daudet's books it was common for the disconsolate French nimrods to squander their time in the field eating and drinking, resigning themselves late in the day to the sport of headgear shooting. The winner was the hunter whose hat looked most like a hat. Latins have inbred difficulties with the value of temperance, Daudet a singular eye for the absurd.

* * *

"Once upon a time," the story is told, a covey of grey partridge roamed the plains of Zair. Among them a small, pitiful individual feebly vegetated while her powerful brothers and sisters ridiculed her, keeping the best grain and insects for themselves. To survive, the little partridge was reduced to seeking minute morsels of food in the fissures of rocks and hard-to-get-at places. Unfortunately, her short beak did not always allow her to reach her food, and she grew weaker.

The Virgin Mary, witnessing her misery from paradise, was saddened and called her to heaven. The partridge curled up in her hand and listened as the Virgin said, "Little bird, I am going to transform you, so that you may know the joys of life. Thrown out by your kind, you will now live alone in the serenity of the forests, where along with silence you will also find an abundance of food. You will be the elegant hostess of the underbrush and will generate the admiration of those who love nature. Your capricious flight and your intelligent defenses will allow you to escape your pursuers. I will protect you."

The Virgin laid three fingers on the little bird's head, leaving three brown transversal imprints now called the "Virgin's fingers." Her beak lengthened, her plumage took on a golden hue, and she flew back to earth as guardian of the forests.

So was born the woodcock, also called "Our Lady of the Woods."

* * *

Juvenal named her *Rara avis,* rare bird, and reading through the cynegetic literature of Europe I found that since the beginning of time woodcock have been praised by writers, poets and artists. Figures of the bird are stamped on Gallic coins dating back to the seventh century after Christ, and at least five European families feature woodcock on their coat of arms. Seventeenth-century still lifes by Jean Deportes and the Flemish painter Jean Feydt depict the bird, as do stamps, money and porcelain since the fifeeen-hundreds. Finally, at least two French wines, a *Chateau la Bécasse* from the Medoc

and a Tavel, *Domaine de la Mordorée*, render the bird homage. It is said that solitary hunting is the domain of dreamers. If so, perhaps a woodcock inspired the Musset poem: "We listen—We wait—The angel of remembrance passes and whispers: 'Do you not hear it draw near?'" By the French, woodcock have always been thought special and worthy of adulation. Unlike our bird, they are referred to as the Lady of Velvet Eyes, Queen of the Woods, Enigmatic Gypsy, the Divine One, and Sorceress. Mentioned in the same breath with some of the most beautiful women of the past, they are thought of as "the lovely suckers." Others think of *les bécasses* as cuckolds.

* * *

In France, as in all of Europe, devoted northern gunners accuse their southern counterparts of slaughtering birds and disrupting what they consider their due. Every issue of *La Mordorée*, an excellent magazine devoted entirely to woodcock, is filled with long letters of accusations, rebuttals and veiled insults, written with the flair and convoluted innuendo so characteristic of the French. It is apparent, however, that there is within the confederacy of hunters a genuine love for the bird, and if one reads between the lines one discovers the plea for bag limits, shorter seasons, and a stop to the slaughter.

In Guy de Maupassant's book, *Contes de la bécasse,* the old Baron des Ravots, who once had been a king among hunters, was paralyzed and late in life constrained to indulge his sport of pigeon shooting from a wheelchair in his living room. The Baron surrounded himself during the hunting season with his old cronies, sending them out to hunt in his place. He then insisted that they relive every shot, every miss and every amusing anecdote at the dinner table. During the migration of what he knew to be the "Queen of Birds," the Baron served one woodcock to each of his guests every night. The heads, however, were left untouched and religiously deposited in a communal plate. At the end of the meal the Baron, holding the beaks with his fingers, personally anointed each head with lard, lit a candle and, picking one at random from the plate, pinned it to a cork on top of a bottle in such a manner that it pivoted. On a signal from his friends, he flicked the beak, and whomever it paused upon became the sole owner of the plate. With relish the lucky guest grilled the heads over the candle and devoured the brains encased in the cracklings of this epicurian delight. The fortunate guest was the envy of his friends, who raised their glasses in his honor, hoping the morrow's beak would point their way. These palatable tidbits were not given gratis. Whoever the lucky guest was had to tell the rest of the table a story, and so began Guy de Maupassant's tales of the woodcock.

The woodcock finally found some food. For a week since the heat wave he had been hungry and had lived on ants, the occasional grasshopper and a handful of beetle larvae discovered beneath a rotting log. The earth was parched and the competition severe. One morning he flew quite by accident over a small coppice and felt a moist wave of air rising from the ground. He landed next to a shallow ridge and noticed a trickle of spring water seeping out of a hole at its base, and he walked to where it spilled on the flat next to a tangle of alders. The sun had yet to rise above the trees, and a number of worms were stretched out on the grass. He fed leisurely, then cleaned his bill with his foot and drank from the spring.

He decided to spend the day in the area and walked over the ridge in search of adequate cover. A short metal barrier impeded his progress, and rather than flying over it he followed it closely, poking here and there looking for an opening. Fifty feet beyond he found it and walked into a hole he knew would take him to the tree line. The opening became progressively smaller and then suddenly widened. Round and round he walked, quietly at first, then frightened, and much later resigned to something he didn't understand. An hour later he heard voices.

He was taken from the trap, turned upside-down, examined, and his band recorded. There was excitement in the air. Moon-shaped objects with light-colored eyes stared at him, and a bitter odor he didn't like permeated the air. He was turned over and over and felt something being tied on his back, something almost heavy. Eventually he was placed on the ground and, teetering under the unfamiliar load, took a tentative step. Tilting his head he noticed a thin protrusion like a flimsy branch jutting beneath his wings. Scared, he sprang into flight.

For three days he felt the presence of the moon faces, and on the fourth he decided to leave. It was just before dark, and instead of joining his peers in the fields he flew twenty miles inland and landed next to a wide river. The next morning he heard a drone and observed a noisy creature flying circles above his head. The persistence of the huge bird worried him, and he flew a few more miles to the edge of a deep forest and hid under the shade of a balsam tree. The drone followed him most of the day but left before dark. Late that night, while he was walking down a timber lane, he felt the presence of a weasel. The woodcock flushed an instant ahead of death and felt something tear the weight off his back. A short, sharp hiss followed him in the dawning sky, and shuddering in mid-air he expelled a long string of chalk. Off in the distance, a young male sang in vain.

The practice of flying hawks is an art that over the centuries has had a variety of marks, ranging from deer and wolves to herons and larks. Even large insects such as grasshoppers were flown at by kestrels. In the British Isles, particularly in Ireland and Scotland, woodcock were taken with regularity and considered excellent sport. Peregrines were considered the best hawks, and in the middle of the nineteenth century one such bird belonging to a Mr. John Sinclair successfully captured fifty-seven 'cocks in one season. The preferred method was to "put up" the bird with the help of either beaters or dogs and mark it down. The hawk was then put on the wing and made to wait on the re-flush. When the woodcock "took air" for the second time, the falcon stooped, sometimes from great heights, attempting to cut it down on the first pass. Once sprung, the woodcock usually zig-zagged for cover, but if the falcon missed, the 'cock usually took to the sky. One such flight in 1886 near Lock Eil was recorded and long remembered. After missing her prey twice, tangling herself in the heather both times, an eyas falcon and a woodcock mounted so high that the party lying on their backs with powerful glasses failed to see either for what seemed an eternity. Finally a speck, and then a second, were observed dropping vertically at tremendous speed. The woodcock fell like a stone, followed by the falcon, who hit it in midair a few feet above the party, dropping it at the falconer's feet.

It is said that throwing a hat in the air at a roding woodcock tricks him into believing the headgear is a bird of prey and forces him to the closest thicket. Closer to home, Dr. Neil Smith of Baton Rouge flew successfully in 1983 two Harris hawks at a variety of game that included woodcock, a 50-pound white-tail deer, two barred owls, a wild turkey, countless rabbits, and a bobcat. A few years ago, Mr. Alan Beske flew a female sharp-shinned hawk at woodcock for two seasons in Wisconsin, catching in excess of twenty-five birds a year.

* * *

For a long time the bird was considered to be foolish and simple-minded, easy to dupe. "Oh, this woodcock! What an ass it is!" *(The Taming of the Shrew)*. One of the first French hunting books, *Le Livre de chasse du Roy Modus,* published in the fifteenth century, describes one method of capturing *"widecoqs"* by instructing the hunter to dress in a short coat the color of dead leaves, to wear gloves, hide his face with a soft hat of the same color, and to fashion two sticks in the shape of crutches. The hunter was then to cover himself with red-fringed leaves and advance on his knees, with the help of his crutches, towards the *"widecoq"*. The moment the bird stopped feeding, the hunter was also to stop and to discreetly rattle his crutches against each other. The bird, finding this baroque figure so amusing, would invariably let himself be approached closely enough for a horse-haired noose to be slipped around his neck! A similar method a century later found the hunter encased in the skin of a cow, whereupon it was a simple matter of approaching the bird and netting it.

In the *Sportsman's Dictionary,* published in London in 1807, the instructions for catching woodcock are nothing short of mind-boggling and involve intricate and specific pruning of the woods, pulleys, buckles, and mesh draw-nets rigged high enough so that "Beaft" might meander without disrupting it. Tree stands were advocated for the hunter, unless "you live by honeft neighbors," and more pruning of the hedges so that snares made of horsehair could be set in such a fashion that the birds were either caught by the leg or by the neck, in which case the "fnare" should be spring-set three inches above the ground. Another method went like this:

Having found their haunts, which you may difcover by their dung, provide yourself with fixty or feventy twigs and daub them with bird-lime before setting them on the ground as you think fit, fome one way and fome another, and if you defign to fee fport, you must be concealed!

* * *

Woodcock eggs were considered a delicacy in many parts of northern Europe, particularly in Sweden where nests were pillaged by the peasants for most of the seventeenth century. In the same century in Hamburg, Germany, the first man to bag a hundred woodcock during the fall season was crowned *Schepfenkonig* ("King of the Woodcock") and excused from paying taxes for the year! A report from Turkey dated 1860 told of two sportsmen killing 402 woodcock, 10 hares, 11 pheasants, 72 wild ducks, 1 wild boar and 62 partridge in three days.

Not to be outdone, the practice of fire-hunting in the southern United States was carried out by market hunters and sportsmen. This hunting method was an old one, common in the fifteenth century in France and described in the book of Roy Modus. The question, "What is preferable to a woodcock?" and the answer, "Two woodcock!" applies to fire-hunting. The location of the hunts was the Mississippi Delta and the great expanse of swamps in southwest Louisiana. The number of woodcock reported wintering there taxes the imagination, but for some reason they were not hunted in a classical sense except when encountered while quail shooting. After dark and after a substantial meal, however, it was customary for the gentlemen to leave the women in comfort on the terraces and, armed with a "fowling piece," powder, mustard shot and a broad palmetto hat to shade the eyes and keep the reflection from "alarming the birds," to burden a "stout negro" with a torch built to resemble an "old fashion warming-pan" with holes bored on the bottom, and on a calm, foggy night scour the fields adjoining the swamps. "Sambo" would advance slowly, the torch burning above his head, while the nimrods followed behind, taking turns shooting and reloading. The birds, visible for up to twenty yards, blinded and confused, rose slowly only to alight a few yards away. Bags of a hundred woodcock, a dozen quail, and scores of lesser birds were common. The women would follow the hunt by counting the shots from the comfort of the house. It is also reported that, quite apart from this sport of the gentry, negroes fared extremely well using cane whips and "threshing woodcock down by baskets-ful."

Even though much was written against it, up until 1920 woodcock hunting in the United States began on the Fourth of July. Barely-weened birds were massacred, although their meat was thin and wanting. An example cited in the August issue of *Shotgun and Rifle,* dated 1842, notes: Two gentlemen of this city, Messrs. G.A.W. and R.S., bagged one day last week in Orange County, near the Hudson River, no less than one hundred and twenty Woodcock in eleven hours."

In the sixteenth and part of the seventeenth century, hunting seasons did not exist. The destruction of game in this country is well documented and looked upon by the Indians with revulsion. A quote from a letter to the *American Turf Register and Sporting Magazine* in February, 1830 voiced their opinion of the white man:

He kills and wastes, say they, without object; and riots over life as if it were a thing of no value. The game vanishes from his desolating path, and the ground is covered by his destroying hand with that which he does not mean to use. The bounteous gifts of the Great Spirit are the mere objects of his wanton destruction.

A more recent example is found in the *Auk,* dated 1940:

On the nights of the 19th and 20th (of January 1939)
Woodcock came into the extreme Southern part of Loui-
siana in unprecedented numbers ... Woodcock literally
swarmed in every bit of cover where they could find
some protection from the wind – open woods, briar
patches – wherever they could find some cover, they
congregatred.

... They got no protection from man, and were
slaughtered by the tens of thousands, with sticks, .22
rifles, and shotguns. They were sold openly in the streets
of the towns of southern Louisiana at from fifty cents to
a dollar a dozen, but very few were taken by buyers on
account of their being so thin.

An old gamekeeper who was not above doing a little
poaching when the larder was empty told me, "Above
the partridge belongs the snipe, above the snipe the woodcock, and above the woodcock there is nothing." It
would seem that although "fnares" and horsehair nooses
appear rudimentary as instruments of capture, they
nevertheless worked. The birds must have abounded
under the English Plantagenet family (1154-1485), when
one commonly reads of banquets serving four hundred
woodcock! Since the Romans, woodcock have been served at the tables of kings and in the kitchens of poachers.

The most famous game recipe ever comes from Alexander Dumas and, slightly altered, goes as follows: Pit an olive and stuff it with an anchovy. Place the olive in the cavity of an ortolan (a thrush of sorts), and the ortolan in the stomach of a woodcock, the woodcock in a red-leg partridge, the partridge in a pheasant, the pheasant in a turkey, and the turkey in a suckling pig. Roast the pig over a fire for seven hours, basting it with a case of burgandy, one bottle every half hour. The host, a gourmet by right and a tired man from turning the spit and indulging in a certain amount of wine, eats only the olive, turning the rest of the meal over to his guests.

Other than a few ancient dishes from England and Ireland, countries not noted for their cuisine, the most awful recipe I uncovered leaped out at me from the pages of a modern "sporting" magazine, famous in this country for its "how to" articles. It went something like this: "Draw and quarter four woodcock. Prepare a heavy batter of egg, water and cornmeal, and after cooking two cups of vegetable oil to a high temperature, dip the pieces of woodcock in the batter, then deep fry until brown. Remove and set on paper towels. In a deep casserole, mix two cans of Campbell's cream of mushroom soup, add milk, salt and pepper to taste, a dash of mulberry wine, and the woodcock pieces. Cover tightly and place in a preheated oven (325 degrees) for no less than one and a half hours. Remove and serve in the casserole. Will accommodate eight to ten people." As this recipe negates the very motive for killing the birds in the first place, why not take it a step further and poach the woodcock overnight in equal parts of catsup, Pablum and Pepto-Bismol?

Extreme, perhaps, but that is not all. In France, and with the author's benediction, they eat the trail of many small birds, and to a decent chef it is sacrilegious not to do so. I have had a problem persuading my American friends of this delicacy, and only a few times when I was in charge of the salmi, and when no one was looking, have I been able to add the trails to the sauce. No one seems particularly interested in the fact that woodcock intestines are no more dangerous to one's health than un-pasteurized blue cheeses, clams or oysters. All abound with active organisms, and in the case of the blue cheese with living worms, visible under a magnifying glass.

Woodcock should be roasted or made into salmis. So declare the great chefs of past and present. I might add that "roasted" in the old days meant spitted over a fire, and therefore the modern-day barbecue would be permissible. Admittedly, the habit of eating the trail, as well as the hanging of the bird, presents a digestive quandary. Brillat-Savarin, author of *The Physiology of Taste*, enjoyed playing with words and used to declare, "To eat is human, to digest divine." Undoubtedly, a heavy eater of well-hung, undrawn woodcock might feel less than divine and probably shorten his life by a few moments, but then isn't it a fact that lust leads down hitherto-unknown lanes to which, against all common sense, we return time and time again with dedication and devotion?

In the old days, Louis XIV liked to eat his woodcock quartered (reserving the trail for the sauce), braised in a casserole with mushrooms, veal sweetbreads, truffles, two cups of fresh beef broth and a glass of burgundy. The gouty Sun King ate well but paid dearly for it.

To hang or not to hang? Historically, woodcock were not hung by the neck but by the feet, and in certain cases not considered *à point* until they ran the risk of impaling themselves on the floor. Ten days seemed fair depending on weather, but a bird was certainly not to be eaten before his eyes fraternized with his brain. Pheasants and woodcock were, and I believed are, meant to be hung. Not ten days, perhaps, but long enough to develop the flavor. The ultimate French method is to hang a woodcock for a few days and be lucky enough to kill another on the feast day. The hung bird is ready to eat, and the trail of the fresh bird can be used either as a paste on a piece of toast or as the main ingredient of the sauce.

Savarin also declared, "One becomes a cook, but one is born a roaster." The Arabs, who are the best roasters in the world, used to say: "Your roast is well enough cooked when its perfume and countenance give you the desire to eat it." With small birds like woodcock and snipe, more than one chef has been thrashed for overcooking them. One is told that woodcock taste like liver because, like liver, pink is within seconds of disaster.

Recipes come and go with time, but in France *la bécasse* is still thought of as queen, and after poring through dozens of recipes from Escoffier, Dumas, Ali-Bab, Bocuse and others, in which directions as far-fetched as the plugging of woodcock intestines with truffles were common, I talked to Faugeron, owner of the wonderful restaurant in Paris, and asked him what he would do if he were cooking four woodcock for his three best friends and himself. "The exquisite flavor of the bird imposes simplicity," he replied. He then went on to say that the birds would be placed, fully feathered, in the bottom of the icebox for five days. Plucked but full, with the neck and head tucked under a wing, they would then be basted in butter and roasted in a very hot oven for twelve to fourteen minutes (ten minutes for a North American woodcock). Once removed and emptied, they were to be kept warm while the trails were chopped and folded in *foie gras*. This mixture would be added to the butter in the cooking dish, the birds placed on top, and moments before serving, flamed with *fine champagne* (high grade brandy). He likes either a Pommard (Burgundy) or a Chateau Petrus (Bordeaux) as a complement to the meal.

A dozen other things can be done with the birds. Madeira makes a fine sauce. Croutons (toast cooked in butter) make a comfortable and tasty seat. Truffles are always welcome in any sauce. But overall, the simplicity of roasting and the elegance of flaming brandy is all that is needed. The bird takes care of the rest.

THREE

It is part of the biological progression that every form of life is hunted. *Homo sapiens,* no longer threatened by the natural world, nevertheless perseveres in the tradition by killing his peers, his motives ideological and self-centered. The rest of the natural world, including those who hunt their own, hunt for food. So much for soul.

Fall belongs to the hunter, if for no other reason than that winter demands it. Energy being a matter of survival, one of the agenda items for birds preparing to migrate or already in the process of migration is an intense accumulation of fat. Small birds on cold nights apply most of their strength to keeping warm and must feed energy back into their systems the next day or die. Hummingbirds, for example, prior to migrating accumulate 40% of their weight as fat, or 2 grams of fuel on a body that only weighs a little over four. Under the best conditions, a flight across the Gulf of Mexico burns up all but half a gram of those reserves -- headwinds are deadly.

Woodcock face the same problem. Light in weight after the August molt, the birds are compelled to fortify their systems before heading south. What is puzzling, however, is that they don't achieve travelling weight until sometime in October. One might expect that by the third week in September resident birds with little to do but rest and feed would be in prime condition, but such is not the case.

For some reason, it isn't until the flights start that the thick fingers of fat that run down either side of the bird's breast and under its wings turn into fuel tanks. In fact, even though the bird is for all intents and purposes migrating, the later he remains North, the fatter he becomes. One might argue that the late summer months are usually dry and not congenial to worms, but I have shot woodcock in Michigan on the first of October following an unseasonably wet September and never plucked a plump one. Two weeks later, having cleaned dozens, including individuals with worms in their throats, the pinfeathers have flourished and the bird has become all but self-basting.

Over the years the routine upon our return to Jim's house from hunting is pretty standard. The daily bag of grouse and woodcock is dropped on the bottom rack of the cellar refrigerator, the dogs are fed, drinks poured, hunting clothes discarded, and bathrobes donned. One by one we leave our mark in the bathroom. Puddles and damp towels, an earmarked copy of Pablo Neruda's *New Poems* discarded in front of the potty, sheens of whiskers in the bowl, and a forgotten bottle of gout pills attest that the paladins have hunted and are gearing up for new adventures.

Harrison, Reems, Chatham and I have hunted wood-cock together for over a decade. We are aware that when we started we were young, and more and more we look at what is left and wonder if we will be hunting together twenty years from now. Fall marks the beginning of a new year, just as it did when we were in school -- it just passes more quickly now. I sense when I talk to Nick at the end of the season that he is at a loss for things to do. His is a short year. Jim is a poet, and his year is as long as his imagination. I believe that what he misses most about fall is the feeling of being entirely absorbed by nature to the exclusion of everything pertinent to the other world. Russell is a landscapist. His eyes see the passing of seasons in terms of light. If he weren't hunting in Michigan, he would be painting in Montana. After it's over I think he misses the freedom to observe without the compulsion to record. I see the year in terms of the months away from my friends. What I miss is their companionship.

It is a pleasure to cook at Jim's house because, other than the fact that his knives are always in need of

sharpening, everything else is available and within easy reach. Nothing that might be used in a stock is ever thrown away. Night after night the wild and tame aroma of fowl and rabbit, veal knuckles and beef bones, vegetables and spices overpowers the house. Stocks are reheated two and three times before being strained, and after they are reduced they are dark and bracing.

For three weeks every fall the household consumes a minimum average of nine to ten cases of wine, at least two dozen giant heads of garlic, and one and a half pounds of butter daily. One recipe calls for seventy-five cloves of garlic and a seven-pound barnyard duck.

Every hot sauce from Shiraka to Fancy Clancey's, by way of Trappey's "Green Dragon," Moroccan Harissa, and pickled Sonora chiltepines peppers, find their way into dish after dish of Oriental, Mexican and Indian recipes. Everyone cooks, some chop, a few pluck, and everyone supervises everyone else's efforts. Three weeks later we all lean towards clear broth, cucumber sandwiches, and apple compotes, but until then we vigorously carry on in the manner of our ancestors. Brillat-Savarin also affirmed that sex is fleeting while food has digestion to anticipate. A statement our wives will attest to.

One evening last fall, I laid ten woodcock, plucked

and emptied, on the chopping block that skirts the contours of Linda Harrison's kitchen. Three young grouse, skinned (a blasphemy under normal circumstances), their breast meat carved from the keel and roughly quartered, along with their legs and a pound and a half of blanched Summerfield Farms sweetbreads, had been resting in a marinade since four that afternoon. Linda finished folding the broccoli purée into a glass baking dish and turned her attention to the polenta. Four bottles of burgundy breathed quietly in the far corner of the kitchen.

It was my intention to cook a woodcock salmi as a first course, after which Jim and Russel Chatham, author, painter and companion in our fall excesses, would experiment with a new grouse recipe dreamed up by Jim in the middle of the night while in the throes of insomnia.

Woodcock, like all species that migrate or merely fly a great deal, have blood-enriched breasts. Conversely, because they live in the underbrush where walking on short appendages is at best uncertain, the birds do so on plump, white legs. I know a lovely woman devoted to eating woodcock hearts. I lean toward a platter of thighs. A classic salmi requires that the heads of the birds be served and the trails added to the sauce, but although I have on occasion presented the dish in that manner, it has never been that well received. On this occasion the heads would be forgotten, as would the mortified innards, but the birds would be cooked as they should be -- on the short side of medium rare.

A *mirepoix* is the basis of many French sauces. It is nothing more than carrots, onions and leeks, chopped fine, sauteed in butter, cooked down in a stock, and strained through a sieve. I have experimented over the years with half a dozen methods of cooking woodcock salmis and finally settled on the method I proposed that night. Using poultry shears, I removed the backbones and reserved them for the stock. After dispatching the viscera I browned a veal knuckle, the woodcock backbones, the hearts, and added them to the *mirepoix,* saving the livers for later. Half a bottle of good wine (red or white), a cup of water, a small bay leaf, thyme, pepper (no salt at this time), a slice of lemon and a few sprigs of parsley were added and brought to a fast boil. I then covered the stock, dropped it to a simmer and forgot it for an hour. While it was cooking I dried the woodcock, dredged them in butter and pepper, and placed them breast up in a baking pan. I then decrusted ten pieces of thin white bread, fried them in a skillet with enough butter to soak them, and placed them on a high rack in the oven to dry.

Once the flavors of the stock were thoroughly blended, I degreased it and passed it through a sieve (this is when the sautéed trails would be added), forcing as much of the contents as possible into a clean pan. The stock was brought back, uncovered, to a gentle boil until it thickened into what is called a *demie glace*. During the reduction I added more wine, a little salt, and a dash of brandy. The moment the consistency of the sauce left a sheen on the spoon I added an egg yolk, covered the pan, and lowered the temperature to warm. In a small skillet I melted half a stick of butter, submerged the livers, and cooked them until they were barely done. I then spooned a can of *foie gras* (domestic goose liver will do but won't be as good) into the skillet after removing it from the fire, and, using a fork, blended it with the livers. Just before serving the purée is spooned on the pieces of toast.

At Jim's it is best to foresee a certain amount of sauce testing by pretty much everyone in the house. Consequently, one should either make a goodly amount of it or be ready to guard it. The banter is continuous, the drinking healthy, and the reminiscences of the day's hunt nonexistent. There is only one thing on our minds, and it's happening in the kitchen. The shots and misses, the dog work and kills, are things of the past and treated as such.

When the polenta was done, I placed the woodcock in a preheated oven at 500 degrees for eight minutes, removed and basted them, switched the oven over to broil and nudged them under the flame for one minute. The birds were then made to sit on the garnished croutons, or fried bread, flamed in brandy, and the sauce poured over the lot.

Crisp-skinned and red at the bone by the time we were seated and served, the woodcock had steeped, become tender, and were uniformly pink-fleshed. Eating with this group is serious business and, until everyone has finished at least one bird, nonverbal and intense. The spell, usually broken by a communal sigh, suggests that culinary ingenuity and timing, given equal billing with luck, have once again warded off hunger and depression.

Soon after the last morsel of woodcock had vanished and the first bottle of Echessaux retired, we indulged in a cleansing swallow of Calvados brandy and plunged back into the kitchen. The pieces of sweetbreads, torn to roughly the same size as those of the grouse, had been marinating in a mixture of milk and tabasco sauce, enough of it to turn the marinade pink. At the other end of the kitchen, on a back burner of the second stove, another game stock had reduced to the right consistency.

Two very hot cast-iron skillets played host to half a pound of butter and almost as much vegetable oil. The marinade was drained, and the pieces of meat shaken in a paper bag with flour, salt and pepper. The grouse legs went in first, followed a minute later by the breast meat and sweetbreads. The pieces were turned once, browned and placed on paper towels to drain, while a portion of the marinade added to the reduced stock was reheated to a simmer.

The milk had absorbed the grouse flavor, and the mild heat of the peppers effectively dispatched it up our noses and eventually throughout our entire faces. The broccoli purée gave contrast to the color scheme, and the burgundy stroked our throats like velvet.

It is rare that anything is ever done right, but when something is and intimately fondles the senses, the French, as usual, have a saying. *"C'étais à se mettre à genoux."* Which means, and in this instance was, "Good enough to kneel to." In our case, and being mutations of artists-gluttons-sportsmen, instead of giving thanks we pitched from the table directly onto our backs, pretended to watch TV, and took a nap.

* * *

Jim and I hunt, a few times each season, a very special place, a place that every year draws an unrivaled and rotating supply of woodcock and by the looks of the cover will continue doing so for a long time. It is a place that we don't discuss in public, and it may be one of the only secrets either of us has ever kept.

We discovered it ten years ago as an appendix to a large hardwood forest that produced grouse but only a spattering of woodcock. It's basically a bend in a river, a spit of land protruding out of a wide leading flat sprawl-ed below a sloping hill. A wide area of the bench short of the river exhibits the black bark of burned pines and a desert of bright young aspens. Three summers ago a fire ran its course through here, and by next fall the section will be a haven for migrating birds. The volume of the river will eventually whorl the tip of the island, but for the moment its flow plays tricks, edging and cutting into the bank, confusing the speed and direction of the water.

At the far end of the peninsula is a quagmire, a place we all venture into once a year, get lost in, and walk out of half an hour later, sweating and cursing but usually a bird or two richer.

The river, laden with alluvial sill, reflects an ochre hue similar to that of woodcock down. In October the young aspen stands bordering the road that bisects the base of the peninsula shiver in the wind, abandoning their leaves to the ferns below. Later in the year the scattering of oak will shed acorns to the grouse. The cover is varied and in some parts dense. Three different aspen growths, a handful of conifers, a few natural openings, lush undergrowth, and a tangle of fallen limbs all help make the cover irresistible to birds migrating to and fro along the riverbed.

We have hunted this wedge of ground before the color change and heard rather than seen the flushes. We have hunted it with snow on the ground and killed birds en route to other parts, and we have worked it when the conditions were just right and walked away with limits in half an hour. We have become, in a sense, very protective of this small piece of land, perhaps because it yields so many memories. Its continuity and reliability are safe until someone discovers it, and whenever we are asked

the lie comes easy. So far, in a decade of visits and some two hundred and fifty woodcock later, we have encountered only one-bird hunter and a handful of archers.

It is good to have a secret. Too many are wearisome, but one that prompts a smile and a temptation to tell tickles the soul. I know this secret place like the inside of my pocket, and often during the course of the year I visualize its every contour. It is going to be tempting to burn it when the cover matures.

The woodcock's fall migration is a puzzling one. Perhaps genetic souvenirs, dating back to an age when the planet's temperature was constant and migration unnecessary, are reason enough to forestall the voyage, but one thing is certain -- the birds leave for their wintering grounds reluctantly. Food and whim, along with normal temperatures, find woodcock flowing with the wind. They travel low and stop often, unhurried in their quest for worms, and appear content to let the breeze blow them from meal to meal. On October evenings, when the footing is soft and the pickings good, some will congregate on the edges of roads or in clearings while others fly twenty miles away. They are vagabonds with appetites.

Heavy rains sometimes flood the shoulders of roads,

prompting the emergence of worms. High ground is the yellow line, which rapidly becomes an irresistible buffet where woodcock queue up to feast and are occasionally poached, betrayed by wondrous night eyes reflected in headlights. At times the blacktop looks glazed under the weight of fleeing worms.

Roads and rivers, stars and instinct, impel both males and females to their destination, but in the fall it is the males who linger. With little else but necessity urging them on, they defy nature's caprices, noodling from cover to cover, and pay for their mistakes by dying. It is in most cases the bird without memory, the yearling, who is most vulnerable.

Legions of woodcock silhouetted against the moon were reported by hunters and naturalists of the past. Flights of hundreds were common. Historically, certain landmarks have always attracted large concentrations. From the middle of October through November, Cape May, New Jersey, was one of those places. Birds would land and rest there by the droves, and even now, on what limited habitat is left, pockets of twenty to fifty birds are reported every fall. A good shot with a decent dog might, even now, kill forty to fifty woodcock a day in certain counties of New Brunswick.

The texture of woodcock hunting is lost without a dog. Through the nose of a good one, the chase and the kill are classically dramatized. The flow of action follows an inevitable course, premeditated and acted upon in collaboration. Charley Waterman loosely classifies sportsmen into three categories: the shooters, the hunters and the dog men. I have been all three but will no longer hunt or shoot alone. My love of the sport demands companionship other than human. I have always owned a dog and would feel naked and ashamed killing birds without one. The nagging aura of indulgence that more and more shadows my hunting prompts the need for a scapegoat. As an active partner in the paradox, my dog fills the requirements.

She's an old yellow Labrador bitch who has outlived three cars and who in ten seasons has travelled one hundred and eighty thousand miles to and from cover. She is not particularly good-looking, and other than when hunting she is awkward. Elevators and slippery floors worry her, and she walks on or in them stiffly, with her tail tucked between her legs. She is easily confused and when so hangs her head like an ostrich and implores help by raising her eyes. She stares lugubriously and for too long into full-length mirrors, snores when stroked, sleeps unless hunting, and enjoys turning over garbage cans. Her coat is velvety soft. She is inordinately deep-chested and used to be very strong. She now is very wise.

My dog likes to hunt snipe most of all, with woodcock coming in third after duck. Fragrance dictates her preference. Years ago, when I used to hunt Lake Okeechobee out of an inner tube, she'd suspend herself for hours by hooking the nails of her front paws through a strap on the tube and remain there, next to me, with her head out of water, until I shot. Her teeth at times chattered so hard, ducks would pitch into the decoys unheard by either of us. I also used to spend the better part of the season working bogs, sloughs and the edges of ponds for snipe, and nothing made her happier than wallowing in the muck and retrieving the obscure little birds. There is something fundamental about snipe-hunting, something to do with the mud and smells, that triggers a basic urge in dogs and men to get down and dirty.

My dog is best at flushing and retrieving grouse and woodcock. Her range is short, her nose long, and she works to cover. When she's working game, her demeanor reveals the quarry. She favors grouse because they smell good, and she works them in a tight, jerky fashion until they flush. Woodcock scent is more localized, and the sudden aroma bends her into comical contortions. Rabbits shame her every time by running away.

A man can grouse-hunt without a dog and expect to do very well. In fact, unless he is using a good dog, he is better off without one. Grouse get nervous; woodcock don't, and without some prompting they simply let a man walk by. The first five years Jim and I hunted together, he did so without a dog, and because mine works close and for me, even though Jim was twenty yards away, my flush ratio was five or six times higher than his. I have also noticed that when Nick Reems and I hunt with his pointing dogs we flush close to twice as many birds a day as Jim and I do with our Labs.

Quail and woodcock, because of their reluctance to fly, are the pointing breeds' ultimate game birds. A good dog, one whose optimum range is fifty or sixty yards but who can be made to work close, one who does not bump birds but backs and works to cover, is a deadly machine. Quail and woodcock are so localized, the cover so obvious, a dog can be hand-led, but the reason the pointing breeds produce more birds is simply because they cut a wider swath without denying the shooter his due. Some insist on shorthairs, others on English pointers, while a

third group swears by setters. The solution belongs to
Nick, who owns one of each. He treats them right, and
they in turn treat him to superlative sport. The breed in
fact makes little difference; the handler makes all the
difference.

The ultimate, both for quail and woodcock, would be
to cast a pointer and keep a retriever at heel. Fewer
birds would be lost, and under circumstances of heavy
cover, the retriever could be made to flush, leaving the
shooter in the open. I once owned an Italian-bred
English setter and a Lab, which I hunted in tandem for
two years. The setter would lie down to shot, and the
Lab retrieved. Both dogs seemed to enjoy working
together, and when everything worked, which was about
forty percent of the time, it was like having a front row
seat at a concert featuring Django Reinhart and
Stephane Grapelli.

I have been very lucky. As a young man I took part in
driven shoots in Europe and have since hunted most of
North America's upland birds. My present dog has
flushed and retrieved ducks, pheasants, quail, snipe,
doves, sage grouse, ruffs, sharptails and blue grouse,
chukars, woodcock, Hungarian partridge, and one
Canada goose. The numbers are not important, and in

my case not that high. What is interesting is that she is a natural, and what she does better than most is adapt to cover. What she does best of all is understand me.

We have done everything together for a a long time. We have slept under the same covers on cold nights and rested on huge boulders that shaded feeder creeks three thousand feet above ranch hands who could not hear our howls of joy. We have killed well, and we have killed badly, but we have mostly been honest. Her coat has lost its sheen, and the years have pulled her skin tighter to her frame. She now looks at me from within dark sockets, and her eyes are aware of things I don't understand. Whatever they recognize, however, will someday become plain to me, and I too will be caught looking achingly at an old friend I love.

* * *

When things are not right, I think first of fixing a bite to eat and then going hunting. It used to be fishing, but for the moment I want my gun and my dog. It makes no difference where, because anywhere I'm allowed to carry a gun is far enough from civilization for me to imagine myself surrounded by tigers.

I return to nature because that is where I feel most

like a child. My thoughts are simple and dictated by what I see. I wander, bemused at nature's impeccable order of things, and I get lost because I follow my dog. The fall colors completely disorient my perspective of time and space. More often than not I feel closer to Mars than I do my car. The forest is a museum, and a piece of ground no larger than a canvas would take me months, even years, to understand. This seasonal return to nature prompts the uncomplicated joys and honest sorrows of childhood.

A month after I laid my father to rest in France, I joined Jim for our annual October outing. My father had suffered, and since he had been a proud man, my loss was tempered during the weeks immediately succeeding his death by a feeling of relief. It wasn't until Jim and I drove across the cornfield adjacent to the woods overlooking our bend in the river that the improbable beauty of the moment triggered my lonliness. The trees, some undoubtedly older than my father, beckoned his memory, and for the first time since the insistent shrill of the early morning telephone call I cried, knowing that nothing would ever be quite right again. My old friend, with whom I have shared almost everything two men can share, was silent for a moment and then queried, "Are you crying because it is so beautiful?" To which I replied that I was crying for my father. Jim looked at the mosaic of leaves bordering the dirt road and at the quaking aspens brushing against the window of the car and gently declared, "This is the right place to do that sort of thing."

Woodcock-hunting, oddly enough, is synonymous with driving. Cover is everything. I suspect that the reason flush-per-hour ratios are on the average so low (2.2) is simply because hunters don't work to cover. Most march into the woods, perhaps beginning in cover, but certainly walking out of it and staying out of it for long periods of time. The earnest woodcock hunter spends as much time on the road as in the field. He stops and starts half a dozen times a day, sometimes hunting an acre, some-times a hundred. His aim is to be flexible and in motion.

South of Traverse City, where we often hunt, the land is poor and the inhabitants poorer. Rampant unemployment, alcoholism and a certain inbreeding have left in their wake a brutish demeanor in the carriage of the men. Their needs are obvious. Survival in our country is no different from survival anywhere else: by its nature it obliterates dreams and defines the meaning of food. It is ironic that within a few yards of these austere dwellings,

defaced by jalopies and junk, short on amenities and long on suffering, woodcock and grouse, even deer and bear, subsist in comfort, well fed and for the most part unmolested. In this region hunting and poaching function at times as a safeguard against starvation.

A few years ago, driving back from a hunt through a deep hardwood forest a few miles out of Kingsley, we came across a figure hugging the shoulder of the road, hunched over a cane, dressed in black and wearing a tall, conical hat. It was close to Halloween, so we slowed down, sure it was a child in costume. The face that greeted us belonged, we were later told, to the mother of four mongoloids who lived in a shack on the edge of town. It was a face complete with sunken cheeks, exaggerated eyebrows, a vermiform nose topped with a growth, and a chin that jutted out of her face. She brandished her cane and scowled a toothless warning before we moved on. It turned out that she was, in fact, a practicing witch who had been arrested for casting spells. It snowed that night and for most of the next day. When we resumed hunting, the woodcock were gone, and another season had passed.

Americans are a people born with cap guns strapped to their legs. They are shooters, unfortunately of a kind whose undeniable rights have also won them the dubious honor of killing each other at a rate one hundred times that of their closest rival. Regardless, ever since Crockett and Company hurled lead balls at the eyes of distant squirrels, gunning has been a national pastime. Americans are the most natural at it in the world and, in the use of shotguns, have attained that status by shooting for the most part an ungainly, gas-operated automatic that bears all the charm and balance of a ratchet. Yet I have witnessed superlative feats of marksmanship by men who never use anything else.

In Europe, most medium-sized towns boast at least one gunsmith capable of sweating a stock overnight. In fact, most establishments insist on measuring and tailoring their customers, regardless of the value and mechanics of the gun. French postmen, usually hunters, are generally better fitted than our most fervent nimrod, the American doctor.

It is the practice in the U.S. to buy off the rack and at best add a pad to the stock. The fact that the individual might be too short, fat, tall, or carry a gooseneck, makes absolutely no difference. He buys it, then shoots it. I might add, he shoots better than his French counterpart, who by nature is not very coordinated. So much for fit.

Grouse and woodcock guns should be well balanced and easy to carry, light and reliable. Doubles are that and handsome as well. Partly because I was brought up in Europe, if I were choosing a gun and I had lots of money, I would pick a beveled-action Boss because I think they are the handsomest, a Holland or a Purdey because I am familiar with them. If I had more money I would scour England for a twenty-eight gauge Woodward and probably never find it. My love for English guns stems from the fact that, between the two wars, the English made guns unequalled in beauty and workmanship. The crudest "bang-about" Holland puts the top-of-the-line Packers to shame in terms of weight, seam and finish. As a test, open and close an L.C. Smith, Fox, Parker or Beretta, and then open and close a Purdey or a Boss. The sound of the breach closing on an English gun is felt in the wrists and pit of the stomach like the closing of a vault. In hand, the guns live like the violins of Antonio Stradivari.

I have settled on a second-hand Spanish AYA because it looks like a Holland. I used a twenty gauge, because I don't own a twenty-eight. My barrels are bored at .02 and .04 and are twenty-six inches long. Twenty-four inches would be better.

Louisiana-born Harry Gudeau is built close to the ground and immensely powerful through the shoulders. He looks like a discus thrower and in fact is a *columbaire*, a thrower of pigeons. Gudeau is a professional and can make a pigeon fly upside-down if he so chooses. He throws hundreds every week and once, when he was a young man working Texas, threw fourteen hundred pigeons in one day. Shaking his hand is like shaking the stock of a gun.

"Shooters are dumb. If I can make them think, I'll make them miss." Harry's lifelong job is making shooters do just that. "I have made good shooters miss by plucking one feather from under a pigeon's wing. It was meaningless, but it sowed the seed of doubt. I could see it in their eyes. They wondered, and then they missed."

Missing targets prompts shooters with the incentive for inventing excuses. Head lift, short swings, falling on one's face, etc., give them ammunition with which to bore the paint off walls. The sobering angle is that unless one is starving, it is absurd to get angry at missing an animal. The qualities and conduct of a sportsman preclude it. Missing is the physical and mental breakdown of a motion that is basically simple: the gun is mounted, the left hand follows the dominant eye beyond the target, while the forefinger of the right hand applies four pounds of pressure to the trigger. Given a thirty-yard or shorter open shot, the shooter should never miss, but we all have, all do, and all will, mostly for reasons of concentration. Competitive skeet, trap and pigeon shoots are won by men with tenacity and concentration. Past and future do not exist; each bird is dealt with within the realm of the present. There are no hard birds, and there are no easy ones. The point is to break them all in order to graduate to the real game, the shoot-offs. Clay targets carry the weight of fervent love and hate.

One of the legendary shooters of all time was the Archduke Ferdinand of Austria, who a century ago shot on his own gun, three thousand driven partridge in a day and another time, using a rifle, ninety-nine Russian boars, missing one. The archduke appears to most modern-day hunters as nothing more than a talented butcher, but when matters are put into perspective, there are shooters who travel today to Mexico and Colombia and run a case of shells daily on doves and ducks. The semantics are important. There are hunters, and there are shooters. The first group revels in immersing themselves in the wild, the second in mastering a game not unlike those found in video arcades. It comes down to a matter of education. What may have been morally acceptable a century ago is no longer.

The mechanics of shooting are constant and, although difficult to describe, are beautiful. A consistent shooter is a pleasure to watch. He shoots with his eyes and his will, the gun being no more than a pen to a writer or a brush to a painter. I have loaded in driven shoots and watched my "gun" kill a double in front, pluck the second of the pair out of my hand, and shoot another double behind the line, time and time again. I am sure the shooter never knew he had switched guns, because his eyes never left the covey. I have shot next to quail hunters whose prowess was more interesting to observe than to compete against, because their motion, the stroke of their gun, was as pure as the presentation of a fly to a trout. Ask a shooter to describe a double he has just made, and more than likely he will admit to something instinctive. Ask the same shooter to describe a miss and get ready for the oration.

Woodcock are not demanding to shoot and take little to bring down. They are not active cripples, and their defenses are passive. So much has been written about the impenetrable alder tangles, the lacerating briars and the overall density of the cover, that to the casual reader and aspiring woodcock hunter the stalk appears a penance, the quarry lost in the recesses of the Mato Grosso, and the target an illusion.

Woodcock dwell on the edges of roads, clearings and streams. They are found under ferns and prefer walking on green grass. Woodcock love second-growth hardwoods, sumac, alders, old apple orchards, goldenrod and hillsides, but they are found mostly in small islands and secluded hummocks surrounded by old singing grounds. It would seem that although the birds live in seclusion, they like escape routes, or at least a nearby path of light. Except when hunting alders, walking up woodcock is not strenuous and is little more than a ramble when using pointers. The dogs do the work, and it doesn't matter if the hunter picks a simple or difficult path, they will already have been there. In the case of flushing dogs, it becomes a matter of anticipation and angles. The focus is on the dog, but six feet closer or further will not put one out of range and will certainly make the walking easier. Skirting heavy cover and keeping a free line of fire by anticipating the flush is a matter of practice. I have drilled a few tree trunks that I never knew were there, but for the most part, unless it is early in the season and the foliage heavy, the position I have relative to my dog leaves me a shot. One develops after a few seasons a feel for the cover and one's dog's body language. Because my Labrador is biddable, I dictate my travelling speed by checking her and sending her where I want. There isn't any point in marching through the woods like a hussar unless out of cover. Woodcock hunting is an exercise in planning, not heorics. My wounds are those of a boy -- scratched hands and an occasional slap in the face.

Alders do present a problem for the solitary hunter. In a team, one member may sacrifice his shooting for the other, but when alone, unless the alder patch is narrow, it is best to hunt downwind and hope for reverse flushes or to skirt the cover and take snap shots at cresting birds. Without a dog one might do well to reconsider the sport.

Hunters should not be denied that the pursuit of game makes game. At this time, game management would not exist without hunters. We pay to kill, and we subsidize nature by doing so. Whatever our personal reasons are for hunting and no matter how they are or are not justified in the eyes of others, it is a fact that the hundreds of millions of dollars spent each year by hunters keep the animals alive. It is also a fact that no one else is willing to pay. Without our injection of dollars, game would atrophy.

The question of how much money is funneled into research and management is known only to the computers. I suspect from past records that much of it goes to clothing civil servants.

I am not against raising hunting fees, but I want more for my money than simply the right to hunt. Primarily, I want to be informed. I want to know the present status of game and the government's future projections. I want to know the number of man-hours in the field, flush-and-kill ratios, loss of habitat statewide and federal, and I believe that my license should buy that information without query.

Woodcock come under the gun at a time when nature's stage is preparing for the new year. A fleeting time when gorged chokecherries burst into lustrous shades of purple and hardwood leaves spin in the breeze. Like spring, there is a bounce to the earth, but this time the assertion of popple and birch mirrors a lustful stigma that disorients one to the point of oppression, a feeling not unlike that of being enveloped in a shallow coral reef. For those vaguely interested in mystical innuendos, the suspicion lingers that one is being dealt a pat hand. The moment leaves in its wake the fundamental satisfaction of the voyeur and the mental weariness attached to the coming of winter.

Outside of Escanaba in Michigan's Upper Peninsula on a warm October afternoon, Jim and I, mildly unfocused and tormented by lingering hangovers contracted at all three of the town's strip joints the night before, decided for medicinal purposes to hunt along the railroad tracks leading to Gladstone. It was more a matter of wandering than hunting and may have had something to do with wanting a drink and feeling we would deserve one afterwards. We had, as usual, no idea where we were, but had spotted cover in the form of alders bordering a bog and, further down the tracks, a pocket of aspen that from our vantage point appeared to be the right size. As sometimes happens when least deserved, a flight of woodcock had claimed the edge of the swamp, and in a matter of moments our stroll took on purpose.

Sweating profusely but detoxifying as we walked, we passed next to an old house hidden in a clearing bisected by a creek. A light breeze ruffled the leaves. The scene was pastoral, and for the first time since the one and only attractive dancer in Escanaba had taken off her

clothes, we were happy to be alive.

The instant the dog got birdy, a woodcock, immediately followed by a grouse, flushed out of a patch of crabapple trees. We both shot, tumbling the birds in mid-air. The Lab retrieved the woodcock, dropping it anxiously on the ground, and set after the grouse, a much longer shot. I don't concern myself with marking downed birds accurately, as my dog is very good, but after a few minutes had passed and she hadn't returned, we followed. The bitch lay on her stomach four feet from the grouse but wouldn't touch it. It had fallen in a small opening beside a full-grown male coyote. The coyote was dead.

The sight of a grouse lying between two dogs, one wild and lifeless and the other alive and frightened, prompted the soulful shivers of vivid dreams. Something forbidden had transgressed that clearing a short while before our arrival. The coyote looked alive but slightly deflated. A thin cloud had drifted over his eyes, but a hint of body warmth lingered in his coat. He was unmarked, but his whiskers were grey. It is probable that he had died of old age moments before we appeared. We took the shortest route back to the car.

The picture of my life is a collage, and within it the

fragmented facets come and go, prismatically shaped and pasted one on top of the other like unrelated abstractions. I rely on my senses to separate the strata. I feel a woodcock whenever I handle a quail and taste him in snipe. I see autumn under the surface of beaver ponds and hear grouse drumming in local tire establishments. Dental braces remind me of birds and the passing of seasons.

A long time ago, before Jim and I really knew how to pick and choose our cover, we spent an afternoon on a bluff overlooking the Manistee River. It was one of those clear, quiet, invigorating afternoons that fall is all about. In those days our daily bags were slim. Two or three birds between us promised a meal, a couple more a feast. For the most part we were grouse hunters. Woodcock were incidental. It was also a time when two-, three- and sometimes four-hour treks through the woods were common. We hunted a rookie black Labrador that year, blessed with a good nose but built like a whippet. She also refused to retrieve game. Her career lasted a month, but I must say, in all fairness, that she had an uncanny and fastidious method of finding and flushing birds.

A few moments after we entered the woods we killed a woodcock and two grouse. Always concerned about the potential "skunk," we were pleased it was off our backs and without ado began to discuss the evening's recipe. An hour later four more woodcock graced our game pouches. The day was made, but we continued on, pushing through the woods and working the edges of dirt roads, shooting well and picking birds every few minutes. We stopped at eighteen, nine woodcock and nine grouse. Jim and I always stop one bird short of the limit. Why? I really don't know why.

When we reached his driveway, we were greeted by Jim's wife Linda and daughter, Jamie. Lovers of game, they took personal interest in our sporting ventures. Jamie was eleven at the time. They walked to the car, rolling their eyes at each other, and inquired about the hunt. We were purposely somber when we opened the trunk, but for once the entire boot of the car was filled with feathers, dropped pell-mell on top of the guns. Linda exclaimed, "Oh, my!" and giggled through her hands, while little Jamie simply stared in open-mouthed disbelief. She was wearing braces at the time, and ever since then young girl's wearing braces remind me of that special day eleven years ago.

We sometimes do things that haunt us with regret afterwards. Two years ago we decided to kill forty woodcock to supplement a culinary extravaganza for twenty people. The menu comprised oysters and mussels, quenelles of whitefish, various salads, the woodcock, a buffalo roast and three desserts. Jim and Russell in one team and Nick and I in the other set out intentionally to kill the birds in two short days. Jim and Russell did not have good hunting, but Nick and I did, so good that even though we hunted only a couple of hours each morning we killed thirty-four woodcock, fourteen over our limit.

Nothing justifies what we did. The birds were too rare for us to hide behind the pretense that they were harvested for a reason. That knowledge only made things worse. Basically, we had killed at random to feed a social event, and it dawned on us too late that half the guests didn't care and might just as well have been fed fried chicken or handed another drink.

I still feel guilty at what occurred, and probably because of my guilt, I remember those two days very well. I recall the cover near Kalkaska, the dogs backing each other under the power lines, the three woodcock that flushed one after the other on a piece of ground smaller than a Navajo rug, and my Labrador proudly retrieving the cripples. What should be a splendid memory floats back like a weary dream, scoured by misplaced priorities.

I will always remember, on the other hand, that during the writing of this book I saw my first woodcock on the ground, not last spring while banding, but this fall, tucked and ready to spring, three feet in front of Nick Reems' German shorthair.

Nick is a master at spotting cover. Coupled with excellent dogs, a sure aim and a trace of poacher's blood, he warrants his nicknames. A six-pack after a hunt may well find him in his bar insisting that he be called "Larry Limit" or even the "Sultan of Shot." A second six-pack has barmaids calling him "Road Kill." Nevertheless, Nick was born with an instinct for finding birds. He owns a tired Land Rover and at all times of the year drives the back roads looking for cover. In the fall he doesn't mind getting out, unloading three dogs, and hunting a twenty-yard stretch, knowing it will only hold one bird; in fact, on his way back from work he usually hunts five of those places and bags a limit.

We stopped the car on the side of the road, opposite a private residence two miles outside of Lake Leelanau. "Nobody home," remarked Nick, "but we better keep moving." His setter, his shorthair, my Labrador, Nick and I invaded the manicured lawn, jumped the hedge and, assuming ownership, marched up the hill. The sun peered from behind a cloud, igniting the knoll and shearing the shadows from top to bottom.

Nick, like most rough shooters, is a dog man. His animals are kenneled but permitted in the house. The boys play with them, his wife Sue devotedly endures them, and he talks to them just as I do to mine. The three males, all different in character, adore him. Bobby, his white and liver English pointer, age five, is constantly in a turmoil and quivers at the sight of a gun. He farts most hideously while standing on the back seat of the car and sneezes down the side of one's face. But when he returns from his morning gallop and takes position fifty yards away he doesn't miss a thing. Cochise, the brown shorthair, is the lead actor. He barks whenever Nick asks if he loves him and works the cover so hard that three weeks into the season the skin above the joints of his forelegs is peeled off. A month later I see bone. Cochise works the middle zones and at six years old knows just where the birds like to be. Mac, the two-year-old Belton setter, is a lover who looks like a dignified English butler. His preference is sleeping in Nick's lap and resting his head on his master's shoulder. He makes his share of birds and backs very well. The puppy is still in him. Nick believes in giving his dog rein. He rationalizes that after the dogs are led a few times into productive cover, they work the rest out by themselves. His only command is "Come!" which he delivers in a voice befitting a larger man.

We wild-flushed two grouse, one on the way up the hill and one on the crest. The cherry orchard beyond the bluff led to a distant farm, whose heavy red barn lay beyond a yard full of white chickens. At the bottom of the hill hundreds of apples shed from a single tree bore the markings of grouse. Chalk the color of birch bark stamped the passing of woodcock.

Walking back to the car, Nick said, "This place is good when the grouse feed, but at that time we're either sleeping or drinking."

Thinking we were going back to the bar for a beer, I followed Nick's instructions, but half a mile out of town he pointed at a strip of sumac growing down the side of a hill that I had driven past a dozen times each fall but had never looked at through the eyes of a hunter. The sumac followed the contour of the slope, bent by the road. We hunted it and flushed four woodcock, bagging only one, due partly to bad luck and partly to my bad shooting. "I've flushed as many as nine woodcock and two grouse out of here," Nick replied to my question. We hadn't walked an eighth of a mile.

A few minutes later Nick surprised me by actually knocking at someone's door for permission to hunt, but as no one was home we four-wheeled it up a cowpath and parked on a rise overlooking the house. The small woodlot sat alone on a barren dune and was shaped like a horseshoe. One of its legs led to within a hundred yards of a trailer. A German shepherd went berserk in the yard. We heard a door slam, and the dog was kicked by a man losing a bet on the World Series.

Nick and I hunt well together. We walk at the same pace, seem to know where the other is without having to shout, and naturally take our positions on either side of the dogs. We work to cover and instinctively leave ourselves room for wild flushes.

I use my Lab as a flushing dog, and with age she has settled her mind about matters. When I hunt with Reems, I call her to heel at the sight of a point, but she doesn't respond as quickly as she used to. Nick doesn't mind. He is very relaxed. I mind a great deal, but on the other hand I like the transition. She used to obey a look and a nod, but now she acts like a willful old spinster.

Nick and I worked the edges of the horseshoe thirty yards apart. Soon enough the bells fell silent, and turning to the sound of a shot I heard Nick's warning. The woodcock spun up to the crest of the trees and flew over my head. A high, incoming bird vertical to the shooter used to be thought of as "the king's shot," possibly because it is not very demanding and certainly because it is pretty. The woodcock fell, the light load parting his breast feathers, stopping his progress and killing him at the apex of his flight. He tumbled with his head to one side and looked like a small pillow, an inanimate object arching through the air, free of life. He landed in the clearing behind me.

We found Nick's bird but were still looking for mine when Cochise went back on point twenty yards to our left on the edge of the woods. My friend was doubting my bearings. "Must be your bird," he declared. I knew better, but honored the dog and circled through the underbrush, leaving Nick in the clearing. Over the years I have stared at a million leaves looking for woodcock and have been rewarded with a million puzzles, but this time the bird jumped out of the enigma a scant yard in front of Cochise's nose. He was hunkered on the ground facing away and watching me out of his famous eyes.

There ensued a time warp of sorts, during which the only suggestion of motion was the dog's shivering flanks. A minute passed, and never taking my eyes off the bird I called to Nick, who implied it might be my cripple. It wasn't, and the oppression finally sprang the woodcock into flight.

I didn't shoot, but, not having been on the scene, Nick dropped him as he curled low around the bend of the woods. We found my bird a few minutes later, lying in the open where I thought he should be. Airwashed, the dogs hadn't smelled him even though they had done everything but walk over him.

A little later a fawn, barely tall enough to see above the waist-deep ferns, bounded from the dogs and stopped, ears cupped and twitching, fifteen feet from me. We peered at each other until he pranced back to his mother, waiting, until that point unseen, under an oak. Together they kicked their hooves high in the air, raced past the trailer and disappeared. The German shepherd barked, the door opened, and the dog took another boot in the backside.

I rushed a shot and missed making an honest double on woodcock, something I have only achieved once, but when we got back to the car we had six more and a young grouse who'd foolishly cut air across open ground. The hunt was over, and it was time for lunch.

I often think about that bird on the ground and am glad the occurrence is rare. It would be impossible for me to kill woodcock after seeing them bundled up like elves in the leaves. I punish myself enough by canting cripples towards the sun and looking into their pupils before crushing their heads with my thumb. I don't know what I am looking for, but what I see is a deep blue reflection of my face. Killing is already too serious and precarious an affair for me to be that calculating an executioner. Birds in flight are targets, but on the ground they incarnate a form of latent freedom we all long for, the power of escape.

A friend and I were hunting under the Crazy Mountain range in Montana with a newly acquired English pointer who at the time displayed all the attributes least wanted in a dog. It cowered and trembled, didn't use its nose or understand commands. We had hunted up a draw on the edge of an overgrazed flat and reached the elevation of the first pine stands. Half a dozen Hungarian partridge, scattered and feeding in a coulee, had been shot but without the slightest assistance from the dog. The birds didn't matter, as we were both focused in on the bitch, who apart from looking funny when she sneezed was totally useless.

We rested in a small clearing on the face of the slope and looked out over the tumbling panes of sage leading to half a dozen barren knolls jutting out of the flat like miniature pyramids. Symmetrical fields of alfalfa and wheat bordered by thin rows of trees partially shielded the ranches adjoining the Yellowstone River. The undefined country beyond led to the foothills of the Absorka Mountains, dormant under the afternoon sun.

My companion, who was incensed at his dog, the trainer and all generalities, but most at having spent the better part of an hour seeing little else than his new acquisition, exclaimed, "This landscape is meant to stretch the eyes, not pinpoint them on the ass of a liver-hearted bitch." The dog was eventually diagnosed as having a form of hay fever and was cured with antihistamines, but by then I was in Michigan, hunting woodcock and concentrating on my Lab.

The business of hunting per se is a narrow one and the focus of the experience too often misplaced on specifics, or worse, on the hindquarters of a dog. The story of autumn is worth more than that. It is one of a river of sap flowing back to earth, a peaceful, orderly retreat to the womb. Sifted from the sky, the leaves become silent museums waiting to be reborn. Fingers of green and yellow scantlings, swampy hollows, and standing pools of dark water illuminated by shafts of light reflect the qualities of Persian rugs. It is a never-ending picture show. And yet, more often than not, after the dogs are led into the woods and the first sheen of perspiration clings to one's shirt, the specifics of the hunt take precedence. I wish I could take a picture that would tell it all, but after years in the woods I have yet to frame it. Perhaps if I could photograph the path of a falling branch, the sound of a drumming grouse, the rhythm of a woodcock's gait, it would tell all, but I doubt it. The boreal forests of fall are impossible to duplicate except in one's soul.

* * *

Jim owns a log cabin in the Upper Peninsula, located on the edge of the Sucker River, three miles inland from Lake Superior. He writes novels and makes war on blackflies there in the summer and hunts out of it in the fall. Russell Chatham and I meet him there in October each year for a week's hunting and usually return for a few days when the social amenities in Lake Leelanau pressure us to attend the likes of Almaden wine-tasting parties and fondue dunks. Nick usually comes up and sometimes another friend, an Australian of Italian descent who likes to eat, is built accordingly, and among other things crewed on the Southern Cross in the 1974 America's Cup. A total of five dogs and four crapulous men in one cabin does not lead to frugality, and our grocery list keeps the owners of the IGA, the liquor store and the two local bars smiling.

Jim's cabin had one previous owner, who built and lived in it every summer for thirty-five years. With the building came forty acres bordering the river. There are four beds, two downstairs on each side of deep armchairs that flank the fireplace, and two more in the loft. The kitchen is small but has a four-burner gas stove, a refrigerator, sink, cutting board and shelves. Next to it is the much sought-after bathroom and shower. Because we have all done it, and because cleaning up after each other is depressing, a young maid drives out from town every morning and rousts us out of bed in order to get on with her program. She is gentle, puts up with warped verbiage, lewd gestures, and is kept pregnant by her husband every fall.

Our days never start early and usually begin in pain.

The normal chain of events goes as follows: The all-important breakfast is either cooked or bought in town. If cooked, it might well consist of half a dozen barbecued rabbits or a huge bowl of game hash, gravy and home fries. In town it consists of an odd number of eggs, fried scalloped potatoes, and slabs of lake trout. Flatulence and potty visits precede the formation of teams who then lurch into the woods, kill under duress and wish they were still in bed. The first hour is unpleasant. The guns have a mind to hang from one's arms, Day-glo hats scald the eyes, walking requires thought and squeezing the trigger courage, but after a while most of the misery goes away, leaving everyone thirsty and somewhat confused.

Our attention span is not paramount in the face of tedium, and less so as the days go by, so we are all thankful that the hunting is good. The grouse population is proportionately higher than that of woodcock, a reality explained by the presence of Lake Superior. Woodcock that migrate to the middle section of the Upper Penin-sula do so by flying east from Wisonsin or west from On-tario.The southern route across Lake Superior to Copper Harbor, even from Thunder Bay, is a long one over water. We find pockets of woodcock in small places, and occasionally the pockets hold more than a dozen birds, but for the most part the cover isn't suited to heavy flights. The grouse hunting isn't what it used to be, either, but there are birds, and they are not as smart or harrassed as much as those "down below."

I can't remember the last time any of us actually spent more than three hours in the woods while in the U.P. Our hunts are short, punctuated by rests, grocery stops, quick runs to the bar, and long drives along the sand dunes and whitewash. Daily consideration is given to a night trip into Marquette, schemes involving the airlift of high-priced party girls debated, but we mostly discuss food. By four-thirty in the afternoon the hunt is over, and the groups meet for the second or third time at the tavern. Famished, everyone is back at the cabin and cooking by five. The menu is never simple.

Dinner is a progression of meals cooked one after the other for four hours. Everyone takes a turn. One such repast, by no means a unique one, began with Russell making a searing turkey-thigh curry and a plate of Chinese spareribs. Jim and Nick cooked a dozen wood-cock and two halved grouse, drenching them in butter, lemon and Worcestershire sauce and rolling them on the grill for nine minutes, while I rounded off the soirée by cooking a double rack of lamb, massaged with olive oil, rosemary, soy and garlic. I baked it in a 500-degree oven for a quarter of an hour and rested it for ten minutes before carving.

By nine p.m., some have taken naps and others sit, Buddha-like, seven feet in front of the fire in a state of quiescence verging on coma. A respectable sportsman would at that point do two things. He would masticate on his pipe while admiring the umber reflections of his dog in his glass of Bourbon and, musing ahead at dawn's bracing promises, retire for the evening. We don't. Courage and fortitude demand a final exodus to the bar, where for the next five hours we play shuffleboard, shoot pool, and after midnight watch the Playboy channel on the newly purchased and only "dish" in town. Women, unfortunately, do not enter into the evening's activities because there are none.

As a final tribute to gluttony, a last bowl of spaghetti and Italian sausage is downed at around two-thirty in the morning, insuring dreams of the most bilious kind.

I suspect normal bird hunters do not approach the art of fowling as we do, but I am also convinced that, although they will outlive us, they aren't as merry. The choice of abstinence or abuse in our case was settled a long time ago.

*The woodcock flew slowly and deliberately, his wings
cupping the northerly flow of air like bowed paddles. Ten
days before he had been in New Brunswick, living on the
edge of a road inside a long, thin strip of alders.
Sometimes as many as twenty other birds lived in the
commune, while at other times he was alone, but there
was always food, and he was strong.*

*He felt good, but that evening he had left footprints in
the snow, and for the first time something worried him
on. It was the same incomprehensible fear he had felt
when the sound of a bell materialized into the face and
then the eyes of a dog. He had dealt with vermin before,
but never one that merely scrutinized him. The repeated
sound of a distant whistle finally broke the spell, and he
flew away. A week later he was in Pennsylvania.*

*The rain had crystallized the night before, but by then
he had spent three days resting and feeding. The winds
had switched from northeast to northwest three or four
times since the beginning of his migration, but for the
most part he had been within smelling distance of the
sea. Twice he had skirted what appeared to be from a
distance huge glowing fires. The wind forced him over
the top of one, and it turned out not to be a fire at all,
but it smelled bad, and he observed entire herds of*

humans and cars coming and going in all directions, seemingly without purpose. Tremendous noises preceded the passing of enormous birds, glowing from inside like certain worms.

He was not alone in the sky. He could hear and sense, even when he flew by himself, other migrations above him. The wind, he felt, had gathered his entire class and was moving it under the cover of darkness to a destination he remembered as being plentiful and warm. Already the leaf-fall was less pronounced and the ground softer.

FOUR

A letter from the Department of Wildlife and Fisheries
of the State of Louisiana informed me that the weather
was unseasonably warm, that the woodcock were wintering north of Baton Rouge, and that the breeding population index for the Central region was decreasing by 3.5%
yearly since its record high in 1979. The letter was dated
December 12, 1983, and signed by Mike W. Oline,
Upland Game Study Leader for the State of Louisiana.

I had by then spent a year analyzing administrative
reports, forestry bulletins, small game surveys and
wildlife journals, and I had corresponded with scientists,
hunters, poachers and professionals. My original, op-
timistic picture of the "well-being" of the North
American woodcock, drawn months earlier by both the
state and federal agencies, was beginning to sour. The
truth is that the Eastern Seaboard is losing habitat at an
unprecedented rate. Three severe springs in a row have
pummeled the nation's breeding index, and southern
Louisiana's wintering grounds, which historically harbor
60-80% of the woodcock in the Central and Pacific
flyways, have turned into a vast cane and oil empire,
bent on dredging the state dry. Specific data, shrouded

behind generalities, lead me to believe that once again the single most detrimental factor in game management — loss of habitat — is sooner or later going to wreak havoc on the species.

I returned to Louisiana in 1984. The previous year the rains which had been incessant all summer and fall had filled the Mississippi River. The flood water had been seventeen feet above normal, and the floods that had severely tested the levees surrounding the Atchafalaya Basin had threatened to blow Morgan City into the Gulf. Subsequently blamed on a whimsical air current named *"el Niño,"* the temperature had been in the high seventies and the woodcock elsewhere. I killed one bird.

The "up" side of the 1983 trip was that I was introduced to one of the proudest and most individualistic societies in the Union. Manhandled first in 1775 by the English, and following the Louisiana purchase by *les américains,* the Arcadians have nevertheless remained fiercely loyal to their new homeland. They are inordinately generous and, more than anything, like to laugh, hunt and fish. When the sun sets on the French Triangle, the custom is to "let the good times roll."

Sam Broussard is a perfect example. He thought nothing of sowing salt and cayenne pepper into sixty pounds of boiled crayfish for an impromtu dinner he gave the first day we met.

A week after I received Mike Oline's letter, a series of Arctic fronts turned the month of December 1983 into one of the coldest in history. I followed the weather progression from Florida, and when the thermometer in New Orleans steadied at twenty degrees I called Chatham and assured him that every woodcock in North America was wintering in and around the Atchafalaya Basin. We met shortly after the New Year. New Orleans was to host the World's Fair in the spring, and in his wisdom the mayor had set about cleansing the French Quarter of the evils that historically bewilder the bourgeoisie. Our hunting instinct prevailed, however, and two days later, weakened but well fed, we set course for the swamps.

Dr. Neil Smith exclaimed, "I thought you'd be the skinny, intellectual type!" He laughed. "Guess I was wrong. Care for a beer?" He surprised me, too, by being the first neurologist I'd ever met who used my kind of anatomical exclamations when distracted.

His fourteen Harris hawks live in an immaculate outdoor aviary, blocked off on one side by a low wooden cabin where food, medication and the young birds are housed. The hawks were in full feather. Smith insists they bear him no affection and only perform because he feeds them. I'm convinced, however, that modesty dictates his words. The hawks never took their eyes off him, flew to him on call, acted pleased when stroked, didn't bate, and preened like harlots.

Neil Smith is in his early forties and visibly fit. He lives on his land, located at the northern extremity of the Atchafalaya Basin between Baton Rouge and Lafayette. The house and yard are filled with animals. His pair of rat snakes froze solid during the December cold snap, only to revive none the worse for wear a few days later. Four parrots and a turtle live inside, along with his daughter's two flying squirrels who, harnessed with yarn, live in her pockets.

We flew three Harris hawks, two belonging to Neil and a young female belonging to a friend. Before the hunt the birds were placed on the scale and declared fit to fly. (A few grams under or over optimum weight renders the birds either weak or sluggish.) The Harris hawk is related to the buzzard family and is an amiable bird. They are easy to train and easy to handle. There were no woodcock that day, but had there been, the method would have worked.

Smith's passion is rabbit-hunting, but whatever flushes is taken, from bobcat to turkey. Included in the pot-pourri are rats, which he attempts to discourage his birds from taking — with little success. At the onset of the hunt the hawks are cast from the falconer's fist and fly directly to a nearby tree, shrub or fence post. From any of these vantage points the birds rely on their incredible eyes to detect the slightest ground movement, prompted by a thorough beating of the underbrush by Smith and his cohorts.

Neil said, "The woodcock were thick last week. Could've killed them with a stick." A hawk stooped, brushed my face with his wings and went on about the business of perching in the branches of a live oak. A rat the size of my foot made a mistake, and the bird set her wings like an archangel and plunged from thirty feet. She crashed through the brambles and struck her prey behind its neck, pinning it to the ground. A few unplea-sant moments later Neil wrestled the rodent from her talons and dropped it in a small canvas bag tied to his belt. He remarked that hawks take rats because they're easy marks and that it's important not to let the birds feed on them. Rats are as delicious as rabbits, and if hawks get into the habit of being rewarded with them, they lose their enthusiasm for more demanding quarry.

* * *

Smith confided that he has a friend who hunts wood-cock at night. "He hangs his Harris tiercel out the window of the car, shines the woodcock and casts the bird. It's illegal, but on a good night he bags eight or ten."

Neil Smith has owned and raised hawks since he was a boy. He prefers them to falcons, much as some men prefer quarterhorses to thoroughbreds, for reasons of muscle and hardiness. He doesn't have much to say about the men who fly falcons except that they dress up and smoke pipes, but he is the first to admit that the birds are beautiful. Having flown all species, Smith feels that without doubt the best for woodcock is the Cooper hawk. "I've watched them fly circles around woodcock," he went on to say, "simply for the fun of it, but they are hard to handle. Temperamental by nature, they commonly fly at their handler's face. A sure way to lose some skin. I know, however, that a pen-raised female, well trained and of a certain disposition, would work. Wood-cock are not the bird's staple diet, though, so she would have to be taught."

I inquired about the possibility of using a female

Cooper in tandem with a dog. Smith laughed. "My birds are continuously attacking the neighbors' mutts. It might work, but not before the dog lost some hide, or worse, perhaps its nose. That's where she'd hit him."

The Harrises spent the afternoon staring at us out of citrus-colored eyes. They flew high and low on wide-splayed wings, walked awkwardly about on the ground, stooped like stones from high branches, and, responding to Neil's gutteral call of "Good girls!" perched, sometimes two at a time, on his outstretched fist.

There was something medieval about the manner in which the hawks mastered the territory. They looked at times like heavy bats, impressive but not very graceful, but other times they pirouetted like ballerinas on clouds of air. The leading edge of a front rolled in from Texas, bisecting the Cajun skies, and by three o'clock the hawks were weighed and put up.

Like so many other things in the South, the vegetation is beautifully labelled. Vibernum, sweet gum and loblolly pines, as well as blackjack vines and honeysuckle, have rhymed for blues and jazz singers and writers for decades. Audubon, for one, sketched and described them as much of the woodcock cover in Louisiana. The birds live for the most part either in the alluvial lowlands or in the piney forests upland of the swamps.

Like its European counterpart, as long as there is a brushy understory, wintering woodcock spend more time in conifer stands than they do when they are on the Northern breeding grounds. Along with pines, sassafras and persimmon, oak and red gum prevail. Drainage sites encourage the growth of shrubs such as azaleas, titi, witch hazel and magnolia. Creek bottoms and hillside seepage always insure good feeding sites.

Further south, the large hardwood bottoms that run adjacent to the river systems and into the swamps are mostly made of cypress, Japanese elms, cottonwood, pecan and willows. A veritable jungle of vines and briar patches six feet tall is a common site in the Atchafalaya and Mississippi basins and in some ways alters the methods of hunting. The woodcock, reluctant to flush, run more and often fly straight up, only to alight a few feet away, a habit the Louisiana Cajuns call "toad hopping." Smaller dogs such as Brittanies and even mongrels are preferred to the big-going dogs of the Eastern Seaboard. Hedgerows, woodlots, swamp privets, and even the prairie section southwest of the state produce at times good concentrations. During periods of severe weather, as was the case two weeks before we arrived,

woodcock are herded to the flood plains and islands adjacent to the Gulf, where at times, confused, they fly over water. Woodcock were reported by the dozens, circling and landing on oil rigs eighty miles into the Gulf the week before we arrived. The bird's metabolism being what it is, it is doubtful if any survived.

Southern hunters used to take woodcock while quail-hunting, but as farming grew and the accessibility to public land shrunk, so did the quail population. South of Baton Rouge bobwhite are a memory, albeit a young one. Joe Huval, a retired civil engineer, was an exception. He always hunted woodcock and remembers when it was routine to limit out on both species in a morning. He now waits for the flights and hopes for the best. Joe is not a pessimist — in fact, his face radiates enthusiasm, and it takes a pouring rain or a barren three-hour walk to discourage him.

Joe's oldest hunting companion is Vin Breaux, a banker long on humor. Vin is famous for his shooting abilities, but although he's familiar with figures, he made the mistake a year or so ago of walking out of his blind with a duck count that exceeded the hundred lawful points. He was dealt with by a judge with a paid-off mortgage, fined, and forbidden to carry a gun for two years, a dilemma that his friends parlay into an unending source of pleasantries. He endures their jokes with a smile and a complement of adjectives directed at the magistrate's heritage. Joe and Vin had taken me to the Basin the previous year, but in a day's walk we had only flushed and killed one bird. Vin had carried a video camera, which at the time he rationalized was better than carrying nothing.

My cousin, Jean de Jean, had once again arranged our trip with all the flair and hospitality his name imposes. His ancestral marriage of Southern and French blood and his love for his aunt, my mother-in-law, a Devillier Arcenaux from Mamou, as well as his position of President of New Iberia's largest bank, opened all doors. The next morning early, Joe and Vin presented themselves at our motel, cracking jokes and sniffing the air for perfume.

We hunted a tract of land belonging to the Gulf Oil Company, but unfortunately it rained all day. We killed five woodcock, hunting the edges of roads and points of land, much as we do up North, except that it seemed odd flushing birds out of palm fronds. By mid-afternoon we were soaked and cold, not to mention exhausted by the effort of walking with poultices of Mississippi mud clinging to our boots.

De Jean joined us for dinner at Patout's restaurant and at first insisted that the seven-course meal, omnivorously ordered because we were hungry, would go to waste. It didn't, and later joined by Alex Patout, the chef and owner, we discussed Cajun smothered woodcock, a dish he particulary favors. A brandy or two later, de Jean responded to our disappointment over the lack of interest bequeathed on us the previous night by Cajun women. Very politely and after giving it some thought, he broke into a laugh typical of the region and reasoned, "In all due respect, I'm not surprised. You boys can shoot, but you are ugly!"

We were in the Basin two days later, but not before we had hunted with Sam Broussard on Pecan Island, next to the Gulf of Mexico. The front had passed, leaving in its trail an ungodly cold that found Chatham and me dreaming of other places. Sam occasionally shoots woodcock on the island, particulary in that kind of weather, but other than snipe and duck we were unsuccessful. From time to time, a figure kneeling in a pirogue drifted silently by, shrouded in the early morning mist, almost lost against the far bank.

The Basin is owned in spirit by the Cajuns. For two

hundred years it has supported entire families and hands over its gifts of fish and fur to those willing to work it. Every day a hundred or more trucks surround the launching ramp inside the levee outside the town of Cateauholmes. The pickups quietly await the return of the boats, but the rest of the activity is constant. Flat-bottomed aluminum skiffs and larger *bateaux*, handled for the most part by men wearing chest waders, criss-cross each other's wakes before running up on wet trailers, gone a moment later loaded down with crayfish, otters, raccoons and nutrea. Cadaverous-looking Catahoula hounds, tethered in the backs of the flatbeds, look out at the world through disquieting albino-green eyes. The men are dark-faced and quick about their work, which must be demanding judging by the wear on their scarred fingers and chiseled faces. But their dark eyes sparkle, and their voices sing in a patois I can almost understand. The hardship of the Basin are shrug-ged off, viewed as a way of life chosen by their ancestors and desirable for the liberty it offers.

Joe Huval was in good spirits when we launched the skiffs in the Basin. While Russell and I had been sleep-ing away the fatigue and bitter cold of the duck hunt, he had flushed twenty-five woodcock. I helped him load and soon realized there was to be a party in the swamps that night. Gallons of shrimp étoufée, bags of rice and bread, beer and cake filled the entire bow of one boat.

Whenever Joe is happy, he snaps his fingers and rubs his mouth with the back of his hand, and he did these things all the way to the camp.

* * *

Five of us sat down to a huge lunch of crayfish. The tails, numbering in the hundreds, had been culled from Joe's farm and peeled by him and a friend the previous night. It took them three hours, masterful as they were, to fill the two-gallon mason jar. Étoufée is a method of smothering crayfish in browned onions, bell peppers, celery, garlic, the crustacean's fat and tomatoes. The tails are added at the last monent. Ladled over heaps of steaming rice, it became apparent that Joe and his cronies took to heart the importance of hunting on a full stomach. When pleased or happy, the men finished their sentences with a soft "Cooe!" When discussing something unsavory, they wrinkled their mouths and exclaimed a disgusted "Ptuue!"

The members of the camp had fished and hunted the Basin for twenty years, slowly growing old barbecuing deer and pigs on their grill and playing *bourre* at night. Every spring a few night herons are dropped into the communal casserole in defiance of the law. *"Gros becs, cooe!* That is the best bird we have, better-tasting than woodcock. The young ones are so dumb you can kill them with a stone. Sometimes we get caught, don't we, *chèr?* But then it passes, like everything else."

The Basin is a deep, dark puzzle. It is a maze of arms and fingers through which the flow of water slowly works its way to the Gulf. The wider channels sprawl against the banks like the thighs of a mulatto woman. In the winter the islands, denuded of color, are stark and thin against the skyline. They would look dead if it weren't for the vines that cover the bramble patches, fall limp from the manglier trees, and hinder the flow of sap inside the Japanese elms, restoring through confusion a semblance of life. The ground is soft and intermingled with shallow pools of standing water. Above mazes of intertwined branches veil the diffused light of the clouds. The vestiges of long-since-timbered cypresses, footholds hacked into their bark, litter entire sections of the swamp like effigies of post-Civil War genocides. In spring harlequin-colored wood ducks fly into fist-sized nesting holes without breaking stride. The Basin's predominant winter musical instrument is the string bass.

The five of us hunted that afternoon, accompanied by three Brittanies of varied origins and a small setter bitch Joe was considering buying. His best dog, also a setter, had died of a stroke the week before. We used two skiffs, stopping and starting, hunting and moving, just as we do in our cars in Michigan. We even winched up the boats on the trailers and re-launched on the far side of the levee to check the area where Joe had found the birds while we were napping. The afternoon produced two flushes but nothing tangible for the larder. The woodcock once again had come and gone.

Joe was upset, although he must have known we didn't mind. The cold front that had moved on during the night had been replaced by a current of warm Gulf air and had incited the birds north. Joe's main concern, however, was that the Basin wasn't holding woodcock the way it used to. He blamed the decline in large part on the sand deposits which had started insidiously when the Basin was leveed and had now reached, he felt, a proportion and depth unacceptable to worms. The sand, in fact, was so fine it felt like clay. It had been four years since the last bonanza, and this year Joe and his cohorts had killed to date twenty-odd woodcock. In the old days the kill would have

been well up in the hundreds. Yet woodcock had un-
mistakably been there. They had left probing holes in the
cattle patties, and the leaves were mirrored in chalk.

Vin Breaux and his friend, who held the title "best camp
chef" of the region, were waiting for us when we returned.
They had brought along the makings of a vast chicken and
woodcock gumbo. I mentioned cooking the birds in less
than ten minutes, trail and all, and their faces reflected ter-
minal disgust. *"Ptuee!"* Joe exclaimed, "No way I could
eat that!"

The warmth of the cabin, and the rapidity with which
the beer and wine were ingurgitated, tempered the afternoon's dismal performance. By nightfall no one, except
maybe the dogs kenneled outside, cared much that the
three-hour hunt had produced a "skunk"; on the other
hand, everyone cared a great deal about the future of the
bird. Woodcock are now highly sought-after in southern
Louisiana, and a week never passes when Joe is not asked
by friends and strangers if he wishes to sell some. He never
does, but many do, particularly the "outlaws" who ambush
them as they leave the swamps at dusk and later on top of
the levees where they congregate for the night. The light is
a headlamp and the weapon a .22 loaded with ratshot. Joe
assured me that the DNR and the federals have cracked

down on the poachers, but I got the impression that over a winter's time thousands of illegal woodcock find their way into pots. The birds fetch two dollars apiece.

* * *

Gumbo, a word whose roots may stem from the word *kombo,* which in Choctaw means sassafras, an herb used extensively in Cajun cooking under the name of *file powder,* or again from the word *gombo,* which stands for okra, another vegetable often used, is nothing more than a thick soup or ragout. In its lowest form, this meal-in-a-pot is a 'ker-plunk' situation in which anything handy is pitched into a caldron of thickened, boiling water, along with bell peppers and onions long since disintegrated into paste. At its best, gumbo is a dish of subtle flavors and original texture, complex and time consuming to make. Every year Joe and his friends freeze their birds for an end-of-the-season party. The record to date is a four hundred and seventy-five woodcock gumbo.

The historical Indian curries and Nordic stews were slow-cooked simply because the quality of the meat matched the poverty of the people. Game birds, on the other hand, are by definition subtle. Cooking them too long, in my opinion, dilutes and washes out those properties. The reasoning behind the two, three, and four hours of cooking time the Louisiana chefs impose on their gumbos is one of blending flavors. I believe they are more interested in the quality of the gravy than on the quality of the solid ingredients. I have fewer reservations when sausage and old roosters are featured; when it comes to quail, doves and woodcock, I'd just as soon bite into something that contrasts in texture and taste with the stock.

I make a game gumbo by building a stock, starting with a roux, onions and peppers, the carcasses of fowl such as chicken or duck, flavor this stock with herbs and wine, reduce it and, after degreasing it, brown and add the birds, but gently poach them rather than cooking them past their original tender stage. Assuming one is using woodcock, the time for consumption is the instant the blood is drawn into the stock. At that point the birds are tender and retain their game flavor, but, as in all instances when heat is applied to food, timing is critical.

* * *

Gastronomic considerations notwithstanding, dinner was a joyful affair, punctuated by wonderful and all-encompassing sporting tales, as well as excitement in the form of a wasp nest awakened from hibernation. The Arcadians found our misgivings of the highest comic value.

The following day proved futile as well. The Basin appeared empty of birds. After a final dinner at Patout's we headed home.

The "Catch 22" of game management is that successful management attracts hunters, who purchase permits which in turn subsidize the management. A lack of interest in a species or lean years provokes a decline in the sales of permits, leaving the state agencies without operating funds. The historical lack of interest in woodcock in the Southern states is directly responsible for the dearth of knowledge available on their habits on the wintering grounds. Leslie Glasgow was one of the scientists studying woodcock in the 1940's and '50's, and his research in Louisiana stands alongside the otherwise peerless works of Pettingill at the University of Cornell in 1936 and *The Book of the American Woodcock* written by William Sheldon in the late sixties.

The bird is now beginning to be integrated as part of the staple menu of Southern hunters, and interest both on the state and federal levels as well as in the scientific community needs only more funding. A question to a Congressman in a state where woodcock abound but are perilously losing habitat was answered this way: "My constituency and I are

not interested in birds. We have better things to do. Just tell your hunter friends not to shoot them, and everything will be fine."

We know that woodcock appear in the Southern states beginning in mid-November and leave, depending on latitude and weather, sometime between the middle of February and early March. Some birds, perhaps more than we realize, and perhaps more as the years pass and their habitat is disrupted, mate and nest in the South. It is possible that some woodcock sing for a time on the wintering grounds, only to leave and resume up North. It would not be uncharacteristic and would explain the disappearances of recorded singing males during the month of March in states such as South Carolina and Alabama.

Cold weather draws woodcock together, and warming trends disperse them. The wintering habitat does not for the most part revolve around the singing fields, and consequently the birds are harder to locate. Light intensity determines diurnal cover. The birds are numerous in thickets, switch cane and overall dense cover on bright days, while on overcast or dark days they prefer open areas. Density, therefore, seems critical to their optimum well-being. Dry weather on the wintering grounds is ideal because of the absence of flooding in the oak, gum and cypress-like forests, a fact that may explain the temporary shortage of woodcock in the Atchafalaya Basin.

The birds forage in much the same fashion and habit as they do up North. They feed on approximately 69% earthworms, 23% larval insects and 3% crustaceans. Insofar as pesticides are concerned, the pollutants recorded in fat samples are convincingly higher in woodcock that forage in agricultural areas than in those which winter in the coastal forests. Some hunters and at least one scientist in Louisiana do not accept the reports of low contamination, and although they eat woodcock, they remove the innards, skin and fat before doing so.

Telemetry work, singing field counts and biological experiments on gonads and ovarian follicles are being performed on woodcock, but research intensity is at a low. This is unfortunate because the results would lead to a better understanding of the bird's wintering habits and, by the same token, of its diurnal preferences. For years it was assumed that 80% of all North American woodcock wintered in Louisiana. Scientists now realize that either the bird's patterns have changed or previous assumptions were false, for states such as Mississippi, Alabama, Georgia and the Carolinas are found to harbor much of that population. Hunters might take note that approximately 70% of the land in Alabama is forested and that studies performed by Professor Keith Causey and his colleagues classify much of that land as good woodcock habitat. Personally, I suspect that Alabama supports a very high concentration of wintering birds and may be, if you'll forgive the expression, a "sleeper."

Our losses, be they in the form of loved ones or simply in the removal of our next-door woodlot, age us in relative and finite increments. The progression of such losses increases over a lifetime proportionately to the awareness we've coralled and will admit to. The intemperate harbingers of our fate are those who, either through apathy or choice, refuse to see, touch or listen to anything unrelated to their immediate lives. The others, those whose thoughts stretch out in anger and who reject compromise for the sake of compromise, those who sense even in their sleep the progressive slippage of the natural world, are the victims, the martyrs of their awareness and the ones whose lonely voices the ignorant choose to ignore.

One of the by-products of the technological fever the planet embraced beginning a hundred years ago is the shameful abandonment of our natural resources for the so-called well-being of man. Nature's portfolio has faltered since then. Consequently, even though hundreds of satellites skate through space beaming back game shows, our seas are dying and our rain forests are being bulldozed out of existence.

The comparative population and well-being of wild things is a lamentable joke. North American woodcock are no exception, but why should they be? The bird's range coincides with a section of the country that has been, and is being, pulped, cemented and drained for profit. Funds grudgingly handed down by the government are being channeled to species of major socal impact, and the starting salary of a Ph.D with incentive to work is lower than that of a garbage collector in New York City. Two years ago federal funds for the study of woodcock at the Moosehorn Refuge were cut off. Had the Ruffed Grouse Society not donated money to the refuge to pursue their woodcock program, five years of research would have been shelved.

I suppose that if one is satisfied with the idiom "holding one's own," and not particular about the wording and its implications, this generation will continue to enjoy the pursuit of game. I doubt, however, if Nick Reem's grandson will bother asking his father to "watch the woodcock fly," any more than my son concerns himself with the well-being of the Calusa Indians. Malfeasance, at this time in history, is rampant and accelerated. Unless we take it upon ourselves to inventory the assets and liabilities handed down to us and use the system to impose our will, the weak links are going to keep flying apart until nature's carnival is reduced to a footnote.

* * *

The fact that certain species do not adapt to a specific and lifelong habitat imposes a wider theatre for concern. Migratory birds are vulnerable every time they land, and their journeys require an accelerated energy intake with no room for error. They do not survive without adequate habitat along their flight paths. The solution to their plight is simple: give them grounds in which to rest, feed and reproduce. But between dreams and reality lurks a balled fist, and between reality and remedies awaits the indolent trumpery of bureaucracy.

Woodcock, like snipe and doves, migrate, are hunted in the process, and are in need of more study. I favor individual state and federal stamps for all three, with the proceeds going to research and the results available through the aquisition of the stamps. I am also convinced that northern states should review the opening dates of their woodcock seasons. Local birds that have yet to migrate are foolishly vulnerable, and they represent the following season's breeding stock. In Michigan the grouse and woodcock season begins on September 15. Two weeks later the local birds are on the move and the grouse less likely to be in coveys. In both cases the well-being of the species would profit by a two-week delay, as would the hunters, beginning the second year. Woodcock need help. Wing surveys and banding are two things we can do. The first requires a pair of scissors, and the second blessedly sends us back into the woods in May.

Next fall, when the forest floor matches its garret and the tangy smell of ferns precedes the flush of grouse, when the first north wind chills the spines of trees and the moon summons shadows from the ground, another woodcock will drop gracefully out of the sky and cautiously walk to cover, as gainly as a pear. I will hunt him because it gives me intense pleasure to do so, and if I kill him I will eat him and love him only more. When the riddle has run its course, I will stop hunting, but meanwhile these hot rains falling on my Southern flatlands finds me yearning for autumn.

EPILOGUE

The woodcock had just finished eating a snail and was furiously using his foot to clean his bill when the distant chime of a bell interrupted his toilette. He paused, ruffled his feathers, walked a few feet, and crouched under a thatch of berry briars. Carried by the wind, the rustling in the underbrush grew louder. A dog, darting this way and that through the trees, burst into view. He looked like the last one. The woodcock kept him in sight, sensing in his breast another sound, a crashing and grunting that reminded him of a rutting stag. The noise materialized into the shape of a man, and the woodcock, not knowing which way to look, lay his bill on the ground and made himself invisible. This time the dog didn't stop but ran in tight circles until he ran over the berry bush. The woodcock's instincts told him to fly, and he did, just as the dog came to a whirling halt. Using the wind, the bird flew straight up through the understory, paused briefly, and, canting his wings, slipped to his left. He felt a rush of air and a sharp blow on one of his legs. A storm rolled and bulged behind him, reverberating and bouncing through the trees, louder than ever before. The woodcock felt his leg drop and hang under his belly. The sound of the gun slowly faded behind him.

A soft rain fell that night, and by morning fog hugged the bark of the birch stand. The woodcock's foot had sheared off his leg when he landed and was lying on the ground behind him. The songbirds remained silent until the mist lifted. It had been a long night of uncertainity and pain, but the woodcock would live. By noon he had applied a cataplasm of mud and green leaves to his stump. That evening a thin line of fire ants picked up his foot and marched it nimbly to their mound.

* * *

Palm Beach, Florida
May 1984